RETURN OF THE BRIDGE
PHILOSOPHER

RETURN OF THE BRIDGE
PHILOSOPHER

James S. Kauder

SQZ

SQUEEZE
BOOKS

Cover design: Jay Cookingham
Interior design: : Jay Cookingham

ISBN 10: 1-58776-152-1
ISBN 13: 978-1-58776-152-2

Library of Congress Number: 2005911414
Bridge Book

Manufactured in the United States of America

1 2 3 4 5 6 7 8 9 10 NetPub 0 9 8 7 6

VIVISPHERE
PUBLISHING

675 Dutchess Turnpike, Poughkeepsie, NY 12603
www.vivisphere.com (800) 724-1100

CONTENTS

INTRODUCTION

I had several objectives in mind when I wrote this book. First, I wanted to record and save for posterity a collection of interesting hands which I encountered during several decades of playing bridge.

Second, I wanted to set forth my thoughts regarding the play of these hands, with the hope that by studying these hands good players would learn to play better and expert players would improve their game and become champions.

Third, I wanted to amuse you, dear reader. In this regard I have added several stories which I trust you will enjoy.

Fourth, it is my hope that the publication of this book will persude the A.C.B.L. to change the way it runs bridge tournaments. No one should be told that he must wait until a session is over to speak to a friend. Nor should anyone be monitored during a visit to the bathroom. Finally, hidden cameras are both unnecessary and insulting.

July 2006
JAMES S. KAUDER

PUBLISHER'S NOTE

In his first collection of stories, the Bridge Philosopher proved to be brutally honest, self deprecating, funny, and good at explaining bridge.

In this sequel, thirty years in the making, good old B.P. is as crotchety as ever, and just as funny. He has some things to say to the ACBL and he's certainly not happy with artificial sweeteners. Best of all, he's still giving you insights into the reasoning processes of a bridge expert.

On demand printing ensures that these books will never go out of print. If only we could say the same about B.P.

Ron Garber
for SQueeZe Books

Hand 1

LOVE STORY

One of the bridge players at the Cavendish West Club is a beautiful young woman. I've fallen in love with her. She's several years younger than I. No matter. As soon as this hand is over, I'm going to ask her out on a date.

Playing rubber bridge, I hold:

♠ 6 5   ♡ A K 10 7 4   ◊ Q 6 5   ♣ K 9 7

Sitting South, I open the bidding with One Heart. West Passes and partner responds Three No-Trump, which we play as a strong major suit raise. I have nothing extra, so I bid Four Hearts. West Passes and partner raises me to Six Hearts, which all Pass.

The Bidding:

NORTH	EAST	SOUTH	WEST
—	—	1 ♡	Pass
3NT	Pass	4 ♡	Pass
6 ♡	Pass	Pass	Pass

West leads the queen of spades and North puts down this dummy:

North
♠ A K 7
♡ 8 5 3 2
◊ A K 8
♣ A 10 8

South
♠ 6 5
♡ A K 10 7 4
◊ Q 6 5
♣ K 9 7

I win the king of spades in dummy and play the ace and king of hearts. West follows to the first heart but he discards a spade on the second heart, East having started with the queen-jack third of hearts.

To make Six Hearts, I plan to eliminate the spades and diamonds and then throw East on play for a club return. With this line of play, I can win three tricks in clubs as long as the queen and jack of clubs are held separately.

Which suit should I eliminate first? If I play the diamonds first and East holds a doubleton, East will be able avert the endplay by ruffing the third diamond and exiting with a spade. On the other hand, if I play the spades first, East will be able to avert the endplay only if the spades break seven-one and East is able to ruff the second round of spades.

I begin with the spades, playing the ace of spades and ruffing the third round of spades. East follows, having started with three spades. I continue with the ace, king and queen of diamonds. On the third round of diamonds, West shows void, discarding a spade.

Before putting East on play with a trump, I stop to count his hand. East began with three spades, three hearts, and five diamonds. East therefore holds only two clubs.

Since East holds only two clubs, I change my game plan. Instead of playing a heart and forcing East to break the clubs, I cash the ace and king of clubs.

East's remaining cards consist of the queen of hearts and the last two diamonds. I lead a trump to East's queen. East wins the heart and is forced to return a diamond. This allows me to ruff in hand and pitch dummy's losing club, so I make Six Hearts.

The complete hand:

North
♠ A K 7
♡ 8 5 3 2
◊ A K 8
♣ A 10 8

West
♠ Q J 10 8 3
♡ 6
◊ 9 4
♣ Q J 5 4 3

East
♠ 9 4 2
♡ Q J 9
◊ J 10 7 3 2
♣ 6 2

South
♠ 6 5
♡ A K 10 7 4
◊ Q 6 5
♣ K 9 7

After the hand is over, I speak to my lady love. "I'm very fond of you," I say, "Will you join me for lunch or dinner sometime."

"I like you too," she says, "but I have a boy friend. On the other hand, I think my mother would be perfect for you. Would you like to take my mother out on a date?" she asks.

Hand 2

A LETTER TO THE A.C.B.L.

During the years 1962 and 1963, I worked for the ACBL in New York City, answering their correspondence. Then I discovered that I could make more money playing rubber bridge than I was earning at work. That was the end of my job.

After this hand is over, dear reader, I will tell you about one of the letters I received while working at the ACBL.

Here's a hand in which I adopt a line of play that gives one of my opponents an opportunity to make a mistake.

Playing duplicate bridge, with North-South vulnerable, I hold the following hand as South:

♠ A 10 9 8 6   ♡ A 4 2   ◇ K   ♣ A Q J 8

East, on my right, opens the bidding with Three Hearts. That's annoying. My hand's too good to Pass. I'm not about to make a takeout Double with a singleton diamond, so I overcall Three Spades. West Passes and partner, full of energy, jumps to Four No-Trump, Blackwood. East Passes and I respond Five Spades, showing three aces. Partner continues with Five No-Trump, asking for kings. I respond Six Diamonds, showing one king, and partner bids Seven Spades, which all Pass.

The Bidding:

NORTH	EAST	SOUTH	WEST
—	3♡	3♠	Pass
4NT	Pass	5♠	Pass
5NT	Pass	6◇	Pass
7♠	Pass	Pass	Pass

West leads the seven of hearts and North puts down this dummy:

North
♠ K J 4 3
♡ K
◊ A Q 9 8 3
♣ K 4 2

South
♠ A 10 9 8 6
♡ A 4 2
◊ K
♣ A Q J 8

To make Seven Spades, I must locate the missing queen of trumps. I wish we were in Seven No-Trump, for then I could cash the top clubs and diamonds before playing the spades. But I can't afford to play the clubs and diamonds at Seven Spades. One of my opponents would surely ruff.

East probably holds seven hearts for his Three Heart bid. Most likely, East holds a singleton spade. His distribution ought to be 1-7-3-2 or 1-7-2-3. Given the bidding, the best play to make Seven Spades is to cash the ace of spades and then finesse the jack.

Instead, I adopt a line of play which gives West an opportunity to make a mistake. I win the king of hearts in dummy and play a spade to my ace. All follow to the ace of spades. I ruff a low heart in dummy and return to hand with a diamond to my king. Now I play the ace of hearts.

At this point, West is void in hearts. West should discard a club or a diamond on the ace of hearts. West, however, goes for the bait. She ruffs the ace of hearts with a low trump. I overruff in dummy and cash the king of spades, felling East's queen. I have thirteen top tricks now, so I make Seven Spades.

The complete hand:

North
♠ K J 4 3
♡ K
♢ A Q 9 8 3
♣ K 4 2

West
♠ 5 2
♡ 7 5
♢ J 10 5 4 2
♣ 10 9 7 3

East
♠ Q 7
♡ Q J 10 9 8 6 3
♢ 7 6
♣ 6 5

South
♠ A 10 9 8 6
♡ A 4 2
♢ K
♣ A Q J 8

Given the bidding and the dummy, declarer cannot have any losers in clubs or diamonds. West should therefore discard a club on the ace of hearts. Not knowing better, declarer will finesse the jack of spades and Seven Spades will be down one.

And now, dear reader, I'll tell you about one of the letters I received while working at the ACBL, It was from a woman whose father had recently passed away. You could see the tears in her eyes as she wrote:

"My father recently passed away. Please publish his name in the Memoriam Section of the Bulletin. And by the way, can I inherit his masterpoints?"

Hand 3

SHORT SUIT ATTACK

Playing rubber bridge, I hold the following hand as South:

♠ A K 8   ♡ A J 7   ◇ A Q 7   ♣ Q J 7 3

I open the bidding with Two No-Trump and partner raises me to Three No-Trump, which all Pass.

The Bidding:

NORTH	EAST	SOUTH	WEST
—	—	2NT	Pass
3NT	Pass	Pass	Pass

West leads the six of spades and North puts down this dummy:

North
♠ 5 3
♡ 10 4 3
◇ J 10 4
♣ A 10 9 4 2

South
♠ A K 8
♡ A J 7
◇ A Q 7
♣ Q J 7 3

East plays the ten of spades and I play low. East returns a spade and I win the king. West, having started with five spades, follows with the deuce of spades.

It looks normal now to take the club finesse. If either the club or diamond finesse wins, I will make Four No-Trump. And if both finesses win, I will make Five No-Trump.

But both finesses may lose. If so, East will win the club and return his last spade. Later, when I take the diamond finesse, West will win the king and cash his last two spades, setting Three No-Trump.

To ensure making Three No-Trump, I must play the diamonds first. I lead the queen of diamonds from hand. West wins the king and returns a spade to my ace. Now I try the club finesse, which loses to East's king. East, out of spades, switches to a heart. I win the ace of hearts and then cash four clubs and two diamonds, making Three No-Trump.

The complete hand:

North
♠ 5 3
♡ 10 4 3
♢ J 10 4
♣ A 10 9 4 2

West
♠ Q 9 8 7 2
♡ K 5
♢ K 9 6 3
♣ 6 5

East
♠ J 10 4
♡ Q 9 8 6 2
♢ 8 5 2
♣ K 8

South
♠ A K 8
♡ A J 7
♢ A Q 7
♣ Q J 7 3

To ensure making Three No-Trump, declarer must play the diamonds before the clubs. This removes West's entry to the spades. Even though the club finesse subsequently loses, West is unable to gain the lead to cash his spades.

Hand 4

A WINNING DEFENSE

Playing rubber bridge, I hold:

♠ A 2   ♡ K 10 6   ◊ 10 7 3   ♣ A K 9 8 4

Sitting East, I open the bidding with One Club. South, on my left, overcalls Two Spades, weak. Partner passes and North bids Four Spades, which all Pass.

The Bidding:

NORTH	EAST	SOUTH	WEST
—	1 ♣	2 ♠	Pass
4 ♠	Pass	Pass	Pass

Partner leads the ten of clubs and North puts down this dummy:

North
♠ J 8
♡ A 9 8 7 5 4
◊ A K Q
♣ 6 3

East
♠ A 2
♡ K 10 6
◊ 10 7 3
♣ A K 9 8 4

I win the king of clubs and stop to consider South's likely distribution. Partner and I lead low from three small, so partner's lead of the ten of clubs is undoubtedly from a doubleton. That gives South four clubs Q-J-x-x. South's remaining cards probably consist of six spades king-queen-ten, and either a singleton heart and a doubleton diamond or two hearts and a singleton diamond.

Declarer ought to hold one of the following hands:

1. ♠ K-Q-10-x-x-x ♡ x ◊ x-x ♣ Q-J-x-x

2. ♠ K-Q-10-x-x-x ♡ x-x ◊ x ♣ Q-J-x-x

If I continue with the ace and another club, partner will ruff the third club but dummy will overruff. Declarer will then pitch his last club on dummy's diamonds and lead trumps. No, the ace, king and another club won't set Four Spades.

Declarer should be able to win five spade tricks, a heart, three diamonds and a club. At first glance, it appears that no matter how I defend declarer will make Four Spades.

But I see a way to set Four Spades. At trick two, I return a low spade. Declarer can pitch one of his clubs on the diamonds, but no matter how declarer continues Four Spades must be set.

If declarer plays a second trump, I will win the ace of spades and then play the ace and another club, giving partner a club ruff. And if declarer continues with a club, I will win the ace of clubs, cash the ace of spades and then give partner a club ruff.

The complete hand:

North
♠ J 8
♡ A 9 8 7 5 4
◊ A K Q
♣ 6 3

West
♠ 6 4 3
♡ Q J 2
◊ J 9 8 6 5
♣ 10 2

East
♠ A 2
♡ K 10 6
◊ 10 7 3
♣ A K 9 8 4

South
♠ K Q 10 9 7 5
♡ 3
◊ 4 2
♣ Q J 7 5

Hand 5

AN UNUSUAL DEFENSE

♠ 7 2   ♡ J 10 6 4 2   ◇ A K 3   ♣ A 9 3

Partner, sitting East, opens the bidding with Two Hearts, weak. South, at my right, overcalls Two Spades. I bid Four Hearts and North, on my left, bids Four Spades. Partner and South Pass and it is my bid.

Playing in hearts, we figure to lose at least two spades and a club, so I'm not going to bid Five Hearts. Against Four Spades we should be able to win the ace and king of diamonds, the ace of clubs, and probably a fourth trick in hearts, clubs or diamonds. Nonetheless, I don't expect to set Four Spades two tricks. Therefore, I Pass Four Spades rather than Double.

The Bidding:

NORTH	EAST	SOUTH	WEST
—	2 ♡	2 ♠	4 ♡
4 ♠	Pass	Pass	Pass

I lead the jack of hearts and North puts down this dummy:

North
♠ 9 6 3
♡ Q 5
◇ 9 6 5
♣ K Q J 10 8

West
♠ 7 2
♡ J 10 6 4 2
◇ A K 3
♣ A 9 3

South ruffs the first heart and plays the ace and king of spades, partner dropping the queen. Declarer continues with a club to dummy's king and the queen of clubs which I win with the ace. Partner plays the deuce and four of clubs.

I could return a heart at this point, but then declarer would ruff the heart, enter dummy with a spade, and run the clubs. Declarer would then win six tricks in spades and four tricks in clubs, making Four Spades. No, a heart return isn't the right play. If we're going to set Four Spades, we need to win three tricks in diamonds.

It appears that I should cash the ace and king of diamonds and lead a third diamond. If partner holds the queen of diamonds, we can set Four Spades. But before playing the ace, king and another diamond, I stop to count declarer's hand.

South started with six spades and no hearts. Partner's play of the deuce and four of clubs shows that partner began with three clubs, which gives South two clubs. Since South holds six spades, no hearts, and two clubs, South's remaining cards must be five diamonds. Hence, East holds only two diamonds.

To set Four Spades, I must underlead the ace and king of diamonds. Fortunately, partner holds the queen of diamonds, so we set Four Spades one trick.

The complete hand:

North
♠ 9 6 3
♡ Q 5
◇ 9 6 5
♣ K Q J 10 8

West
♠ 7 2
♡ J 10 6 4 2
◇ A K 3
♣ A 9 3

East
♠ Q 5
♡ A K 9 8 7 3
◇ Q 7
♣ 7 4 2

South
♠ A K J 10 8 4
♡ —
◇ J 10 8 4 2
♣ 6 5

I got off to a poor opening lead. On the auction, it's likely that East holds a doubleton spade and six hearts. East's remaining cards should be two diamonds and three clubs or three diamonds and two clubs. A diamond lead is better than a heart, for East may be able to ruff the third round of diamonds.

Hand 6

ASSISTANCE FROM THE DEFENSE

When playing bridge, it's frequently a good idea to give your opponents an opportunity to make a mistake. Hands that should be set may be made with an opponent's help. Consider this hand, where West misdefends and allows declarer to make Three No-Trump:

The Bidding:

NORTH	EAST	SOUTH	WEST
—	—	1NT	Pass
3NT	Pass	Pass	Pass

North
♠ A 5 4
♡ 7 4 2
♢ 6 5 4
♣ A Q 4 2

South
♠ K 7 3
♡ A K 6 3
♢ A 8 7 3
♣ K 7

West leads the queen of spades.

I have eight top tricks. If the hearts break three-three, I can make Three No-Trump. Normally, it would be correct to duck the first spade. However, if I duck the first spade, then a diamond shift might set Three No-Trump even when the hearts are breaking three-three. In addition, if

I allow West to win his spades, I may later be able to squeeze East in hearts and clubs. I therefore win the king of spades in hand and lead a low heart.

East wins the first heart and returns a spade, which I win in dummy. There is no need to test the hearts now. If the hearts are breaking three-three, I'll always make Three No-Trump. Meanwhile, I return a spade, giving West the opportunity to win his remaining spades.

Sure enough, West wins the third round of spades and cashes two more spades. Dummy and I pitch diamonds on the fourth and fifth round of spades. East, meanwhile, pitches a club and two diamonds.

This is the position when West exits with the king of diamonds to my ace:

North
♠ —
♡ 7 4
◊ 6
♣ A Q 4 2

West
♠ —
♡ J
◊ K Q 9 2
♣ 8 3

East
♠ —
♡ Q 10 9
◊ —
♣ J 10 9 6

South
♠ —
♡ A K 6
◊ A 8
♣ K 7

East is squeezed as I win the ace of diamonds. If he discards a heart, I'll win three tricks in hearts. And if East discards a club, then I will win four tricks in clubs. With West's help, I make Three No-Trump.

The complete hand:

North
♠ A 5 4
♡ 7 4 2
◇ 6 5 4
♣ A Q 4 2

West
♠ Q J 10 8 6
♡ J 5
◇ K Q 9 2
♣ 8 3

East
♠ 9 2
♡ Q 10 9 8
◇ J 10
♣ J 10 9 6 5

South
♠ K 7 3
♡ A K 6 3
◇ A 8 7 3
♣ K 7

Three No-Trump should be set. After winning the third round of spades, West should play the king of diamonds. If declarer ducks the king of diamonds, West cashes his remaining spades. If declarer wins the ace of diamonds, then East can hold both clubs and hearts and no squeeze occurs.

Hand 7

THE DINOSAUR

When I went to college, no one owned a calculator. Instead, we had slide rules. Likewise, no one owned a computer, a cordless telephone, nor a VCR. All of these products came into existence after my college years.

Bridge too has changed since my college years. Hundreds of new conventions have come into existence. But the play of the hand remains the same.

Partner and I bid to Six Spades on the following hand:

The Bidding:

NORTH	EAST	SOUTH	WEST
1 ◇	Pass	1 ♠	Pass
2 ♠	Pass	4NT	Pass
5 ♡	Pass	5NT	Pass
6 ◇	Pass	6 ♠	Pass
Pass	Pass		

West leads the jack of hearts and North puts down this dummy:

North
♠ A 9 3
♡ 7 4
◇ J 10 9 6 5
♣ A K J

South
♠ K J 8 4 2
♡ A K
◇ A Q
♣ Q 10 4 3

Wrong contract! We belong in Six No-Trump. But I should be able to make Six Spades if the diamond finesse wins or the spades break three-two, with the queen of spades at my right.

I win the queen of hearts with the king and lead a club to dummy's ace. I then try the diamond finesse, which wins. Since I have no diamond losers, I can afford a safety play in spades. I cash the king of spades and all follow. Next, I lead a spade toward dummy. West plays low and I play dummy's nine.

If East is able to win the nine of spades, then the spades will be breaking three-two and I will have twelve tricks. East, however, shows out of spades, dummy's nine winning. I cash dummy's ace of spades and later concede a trump trick to West's queen, making Six Spades.

The complete hand:

North
♠ A 9 3
♡ 7 4
◇ J 10 9 6 5
♣ A K J

West
♠ Q 10 7 5
♡ J 10 9 3
◇ 7 4
♣ 9 7 5

East
♠ 6
♡ Q 8 6 5 2
◇ K 8 3 2
♣ 8 6 2

South
♠ K J 8 4 2
♡ A K
◇ A Q
♣ Q 10 4 3

Declarer should take the diamond finesse early. If the diamond finesse wins, declarer safety-plays the spades. If the diamond finesse loses, then declarer must play a spade to dummy's ace and finesse the jack of spades.

East, of course, might win the second round of spades and give West a ruff in diamonds or clubs. But I still think the best play is to take the diamond finesse early and then safety play the spades, for a four-one spade split is a far greater threat than a five-one split in the minors.

After several hours of rubber bridge, I return to my condo and begin reading a book on Computers For Dummies. It's too difficult. After an hour I give up. I turn off my computer and put the book away, feeling like a dinosaur from another age.

But I'm not discouraged. At least I've mastered the use of the remote control for my television set.

Hand 8

CREATING A GUESS

Playing rubber bridge, I find myself defending Four Spades on the following hand:

The Bidding:

NORTH	EAST	SOUTH	WEST
1 ♣	Pass	1 ♠	Pass
2NT	Pass	3 ♣	Pass
3 ♠	Pass	4 ♠	Pass
Pass	Pass		

North
- ♠ K 5 4
- ♡ J 9 3
- ◊ A K 3
- ♣ A K J 9

East
- ♠ 7 2
- ♡ A 10 8 2
- ◊ J 9 6 5
- ♣ 7 6 3

Partner leads the king and queen of hearts and continues with a third heart to my ace, which wins, declarer having started with three hearts.

On the auction, South ought to have five spades and four clubs. South's most likely distribution is 5-3-1-4. Since dummy has the ace and king of diamonds and the ace, king and jack of clubs, it's obvious that the defense will not win a trick in either diamonds or clubs. To set Four Spades, it's necessary for the defense to win a trump trick.

If partner holds the Q-10-x of spades, we'll always win a trump trick. But declarer may hold the A-Q-x-x-x of spades. With the spades breaking three-two, the defense will not be able to win a trump trick.

I see a chance, however, to win a trump trick if partner holds either the J-10-x or J-9-x of spades. I can put declarer to a guess by returning a heart for partner to ruff with the nine or ten of spades. Sure enough, this is the complete hand:

North
♠ K 5 4
♡ J 9 3
◇ A K 3
♣ A K J 9

West
♠ J 9 6
♡ K Q 6
◇ Q 10 8 4 2
♣ 5 2

East
♠ 7 2
♡ A 10 8 2
◇ J 9 6 5
♣ 7 6 3

South
♠ A Q 10 8 3
♡ 7 5 4
◇ 7
♣ Q 10 8 4

South ruffs the heart in hand with the eight of spades, partner overruffs with the nine and North wins with the king. Declarer leads a spade to his ace and then enters dummy with a diamond. Declarer leads another spade and finesses the ten. Partner wins the jack of spades, so Four Spades is down one.

Hand 9

A PITCH ON THE RIGHT SUIT

Playing rubber bridge, I hold the following hand as South:

♠ 4 2   ♡ A K 9 8 7 2   ◊ K Q 7   ♣ 7 3

I open the bidding with One Heart. West passes and partner responds One Spade. East Passes and I rebid Two Hearts. West Passes and North raises me to Six Hearts, which all Pass.

The Bidding:

NORTH	EAST	SOUTH	WEST
—	—	1 ♡	Pass
1 ♠	Pass	2 ♡	Pass
6 ♡	Pass	Pass	Pass

West leads the queen of clubs and North puts down this dummy:

North
♠ A Q J 8 7 3
♡ 10 4 3
◊ A 6
♣ A 9

South
♠ 4 2
♡ A K 9 8 7 2
◊ K Q 7
♣ 7 3

Six Hearts is an excellent contract. I can make Six Hearts if the hearts break two-two or if the spade finesse wins.

I win the ace of clubs and play the ace and king of hearts. East follows to the first heart, but on the second heart he discards a diamond, West having started with the queen-jack third of hearts.

It looks normal now to play the ace, king and queen of diamonds, to pitch dummy's club loser. However, I see a problem with playing the diamonds early. If West began with a doubleton diamond, West would ruff the third round of diamonds and lead a club. After ruffing the club, I would be stuck in dummy and forced to lead away from dummy's ace-queen of spades.

With West holding a trump trick, I can't make Six Hearts unless the spade finesse wins. I take the spade finesse early, without playing the diamonds for a club pitch. If the spade finesse loses, I will be down two, but if the spade finesse wins, I should be able to make Six Hearts.

Fortunately, the spade finesse wins. I could play the diamonds now, to pitch dummy's club, but since West must hold the king of spades, I decide to take another spade finesse for a club pitch from hand. I lead a diamond to my king and continue with a second spade to dummy's jack, which wins. I then pitch my club loser on dummy's ace of spades, making Six Hearts.

My precautions were necessary, for this was the complete hand:

North
♠ A Q J 8 7 3
♥ 10 4 3
♦ A 6
♣ A 9

West
♠ K 10 9 5
♥ Q J 6
♦ 3
♣ Q J 10 4 2

East
♠ 6
♥ 5
♦ J 10 9 8 5 4 2
♣ K 8 6 5

South
♠ 4 2
♥ A K 9 8 7 2
♦ K Q 7
♣ 7 3

If declarer attempts to pitch dummy's club loser on the third round of diamonds, West ruffs the second diamond and cashes a club. Once the spade finesse wins, West is marked with the king of spades. It's therefore correct to take the spade finesse again rather than play the diamonds.

Oddly enough, West might set Six Hearts if he plays the king of spades on the first lead. If declarer believes the king of spades is singleton, declarer will play the diamonds for a club pitch.

Hand 10

THE SINGLE MAN

Playing rubber bridge, I hold the following hand as South:

♠ A K 8   ♡ A K 4 2   ◊ 10 8   ♣ A K Q 4

Partner and I bid to Three No-Trump on the following auction:

NORTH	EAST	SOUTH	WEST
Pass	Pass	2 ♣*	Pass
2 ◊**	Pass	2NT	Pass
3NT	Pass	Pass	Pass

*strong and artificial   **less than 8 hcp

West leads the queen of hearts and partner puts down this dummy:

North
♠ 5 3 2
♡ 9 6 5
◊ K Q J 9 6
♣ 7 5

South
♠ A K 8
♡ A K 4 2
◊ 10 8
♣ A K Q 4

I have eight top tricks, consisting of two spades, two hearts, a diamond and three clubs. If the hearts break three-three, I can win another trick in hearts. But with West leading the queen of hearts, it's likely that the hearts will break four-two rather than three-three.

I can win two tricks in diamonds if the opponent with the ace of diamonds ducks twice. But my opponents aren't that nice. They'll duck the first diamond and win the second diamond. How am I going to win nine tricks?

I see a chance to win a second diamond trick. If I duck a spade and cash all of my winners, I can strip the hand holding the ace of diamonds of all exit cards. Then if the opponent with the ace of diamonds holds three or more diamonds, I will win a second trick in diamonds.

I win the queen of hearts with the king and play a low spade from hand, which West wins with the nine. West continues with the jack of hearts which I win with the ace, East following.

I lead the eight of diamonds to dummy's king, which holds. I then cash the ace and king of spades and the ace, king and queen of clubs. Next, I lead a second diamond which East wins with the ace.

At this point, my opponents have won a spade and the ace of diamonds. They have two hearts, a spade, and a club to cash, but no way to gain entry back and forth to win all these tricks.

After winning the ace of diamonds, East cashes a high spade and a high club. Fortunately, East's last card is a diamond which I win in dummy, so I make Three No-Trump.

The complete hand:

North
♠ 5 3 2
♡ 9 6 5
◊ K Q J 9 6
♣ 7 5

West
♠ J 9 6
♡ Q J 10 8
◊ 7 5 4
♣ 9 3 2

East
♠ Q 10 7 4
♡ 7 3
◊ A 3 2
♣ J 10 8 6

South
♠ A K 8
♡ A K 4 2
◊ 10 8
♣ A K Q 4

If declarer ducks the first heart, East pitches a low diamond on the third heart and Three No-Trump is down one.

With the line of play which I adopted, Three No-Trump makes when West holds the ace of diamonds and West's distribution is 3-4-3-3, 3-4-4-2, or 2-4-4-3. Three No-Trump also makes when East holds the ace of diamonds and his distribution is 5-2-3-3, 4-2-4-3, 4-2-3-4, or 3-2-4-4.

Normally, our Saturday night rubber bridge game ends at midnight. But tonight the other players ask me to play until two a.m. "I can play another two hours," I say. And why not? There's no one at home waiting for me.

Hand 11

A MIDNIGHT COMPANION

This bridge hand came from the Denver Nationals more than twenty years ago. On my first day, during the evening session, I run into Bob, a friend of mine from San Francisco. We agree to meet after the session is over.

How should declarer play to make Six No-Trump on the following hand?

The Bidding:

NORTH	EAST	SOUTH	WEST
—	—	1NT	Pass
6NT	Pass	Pass	Pass

North
- ♠ A 7 6 5
- ♡ A 8 3
- ♢ K 7 6
- ♣ A J 5

South
- ♠ K 8 3
- ♡ Q 4
- ♢ A Q 2
- ♣ K Q 10 9 6

Opening lead: Jack of diamonds

Declarer begins with two tricks in spades, one trick in hearts, three diamonds and five clubs, for a total of eleven tricks.

Playing the spades succeeds when the spades break three-three. Leading a heart toward the queen succeeds if East holds the king of hearts.

A three-three spade break occurs only 36% of the time. Leading a heart to the queen succeeds 50% of the time. At first sight, the heart finesse appears to be the better play.

But Six No-Trump can also be made on a squeeze whenever the defender with the length in spades holds the king of hearts. If the spades break four-two, the player with four spades will hold the king of hearts 45% of the time. The combined chances of a three-three spade break and a squeeze are approximately 64%.

Playing for a spade break or a squeeze is clearly better than leading toward the queen of hearts, for leading toward the queen of hearts has only a 50% chance of success. Declarer should therefore win the diamond and duck a spade. Declarer wins any return, cashes the ace of hearts, and runs the diamonds and clubs to arrive at this position:

North
♠ A 7 6
♡ 3
◇ —
♣ —

West
♠ Q 10 9
♡ K
◇ —
♣ —

East
♠ J
♡ J 9 7
◇ —
♣ —

South
♠ K 3
♡ Q
◇ —
♣ 6

The last club squeezes West, who holds both the spades and the king of hearts. If West discards a spade, then declarer runs the spades. If West discards the king of hearts, then declarer wins the queen of hearts. This squeeze also works if East holds the spades and the king of hearts.

The complete hand:

North
- ♠ A 7 6 5
- ♡ A 8 3
- ◇ K 7 6
- ♣ A J 5

West
- ♠ Q 10 9 2
- ♡ K 10 5
- ◇ J 10 9 5
- ♣ 7 4

East
- ♠ J 4
- ♡ J 9 7 6 2
- ◇ 8 4 3
- ♣ 8 3 2

South
- ♠ K 8 3
- ♡ Q 4
- ◇ A Q 2
- ♣ K Q 10 9 6

"Jim, you've got to help me," says my friend Bob. "I've fallen in love with a girl named Rosemary, from Seattle, and I know she loves me too. The trouble is that her roommate Betty never lets us be alone."

"What can I do to help?" I ask

"Make a play for her roommate," asks Bob.

"All right," I reply.

Bob and I meet the girls in the hotel coffee shop, where we have a late dinner. During the meal, I tell Betty how attractive I find her. I manage to separate Betty from Rosemary. Meanwhile Bob and Rosemary leave together.

The next morning, I ask Bob how things went with Rosemary.

"Very well," He tells me. "She spent the night in my room."

I congratuate Bob on his good fortune. I never tell Bob that I also had a Midnight Companion.

Hand 12

WHAT PEOPLE THINK

Playing in a Regional bridge tournament, I hold:

♠ A 2   ♡ J 5 4   ♢ Q 10 7 6   ♣ A K 4 3

North, on my left, opens the bidding with One Club. Partner Passes and South bids One Spade. I Pass and North bids Two Spades. Partner Passes and South bids Four Spades, which all Pass.

The Bidding:

NORTH	EAST	SOUTH	WEST
1 ♣	Pass	1 ♠	Pass
2 ♠	Pass	4 ♠	Pass
Pass	Pass		

I lead the king of clubs and North puts down this dummy:

          North
          ♠ Q 7 6 5
          ♡ K 6
          ♢ A 8 3
          ♣ Q J 10 8

West
♠ A 2
♡ J 5 4
♢ Q 10 7 6
♣ A K 4 3

Partner plays the deuce of clubs, showing three. From the bidding, declarer ought to have four or five spades to the king-jack, the ace of hearts and the king of diamonds. At first glance, it appears that the defense will be limited to two clubs and a spade.

In order to set Four Spades, it will be necessary to win a trick in diamonds. It looks correct, therefore, to shift to a diamond. But if declarer's distribution is 5-3-3-2, he will win the first diamond and play a club, win the second diamond and pitch a diamond on dummy's clubs, losing only three tricks.

In short, if declarer's distribution is 5-3-3-2, Four Spades cannot be set. But if South's distribution is 4-3-4-2 or 5-2-4-2, it's possible to set Four Spades. If I lead a diamond and partner holds the jack, the defense will be able to win a diamond before declarer can discard two diamonds on dummy's clubs. However, a diamond shift would be disastrous if declarer held the K-J-x-x of diamonds.

I see a way, however, to set Four Spades without risking a diamond lead away from my queen. I continue with the ace of clubs and a third club which dummy wins with the jack, declarer pitching a diamond.

Declarer leads a spade to his king and my ace. I then lead a fourth round of clubs, which partner ruffs low and declarer overruffs. South's distribution is 5-2-4-2, as I had hoped. Declarer is later forced to take a diamond finesse, which loses, so Four Spades is down one.

The complete hand:

North
♠ Q 7 6 5
♡ K 6
◇ A 8 3
♣ Q J 10 8

West
♠ A 2
♡ J 5 4
◇ Q 10 7 6
♣ A K 4 3

East
♠ 8 4
♡ Q 10 8 7 3 2
◇ 9 4
♣ 9 6 2

South
♠ K J 10 9 3
♡ A 9
◇ K J 5 2
♣ 7 5

If West fails to play the ace, king and another club, and later a fourth club for East to ruff, then declarer will be able to pitch two diamonds on dummy's clubs.

After the round is called, partner and I move to the next table, but they have not finished playing the round. We wait nearby, for the hand to be completed and scored.

The director comes by and advises us to move away from the table. "Otherwise," says the director, "People will think that you are cheating by watching hands which you have yet to play."

Partner and I comply with the director's wishes and move away from the table. But I can't help wonder. Do people really think that you're cheating when you stand near a table where a hand is being played?

Hand 13

THE DUMPER

When playing rubber bridge, I prefer to play against dumpers. A "dumper" is a very weak bridge player, one with far less than ordinary skills. Once in a while, however, I shift gears and become the dumper.

Sitting East, I hold:

♠ A 4 2   ♡ A K 8 7 6   ◇ 2   ♣ K J 8 3

I open the bidding with One Heart and South overcalls One Spade. Partner competes with Two Hearts and North makes a limit raise of Three Spades.

On the auction, it's likely that partner holds a singleton spade. If so, Four Hearts will make if partner holds as little as the queen of hearts and the queen of clubs. Whatever partner's hand may be, I should have a good play for game, so I bid Four Hearts. South, however, bids Four Spades. West and North Pass and I Double. All Pass, so the bidding has been:

NORTH	EAST	SOUTH	WEST
—	1 ♡	1 ♠	2 ♡
3 ♠	4 ♡	4 ♠	Pass
Pass	Dbl	Pass	Pass
Pass			

Partner leads the queen of hearts and North puts down this dummy:

North
♠ J 10 9 3
♡ 5 2
◊ A Q 10 6 4
♣ 7 6

East
♠ A 4 2
♡ A K 8 7 6
◊ 2
♣ K J 8 3

I win the king of hearts. Holding the ace third of spades, it appears best to play for a diamond ruff. I therefore return the deuce of diamonds which declarer wins in dummy with the ten. Declarer plays a club to his queen, which holds, and continues with the ace and nine of clubs, pitching a heart from dummy. I win the jack of clubs, but I am unable now to put partner on lead for a diamond ruff. Declarer later picks up my trumps, making Four Spades, Doubled.

The complete hand:

North
♠ J 10 9 3
♡ 5 2
◊ A Q 10 6 4
♣ 7 6

West
♠ 7
♡ Q J 10 3
◊ J 9 8 5
♣ 10 5 4 2

East
♠ A 4 2
♡ A K 8 7 6
◊ 2
♣ K J 8 3

South
♠ K Q 8 6 5
♡ 9 4
◊ K 7 3
♣ A Q 9

Four Spades can be set. I should have played the jack of clubs under the ace. West could then cover the nine of clubs with the ten, to gain the lead in case dummy pitches a heart on the third club. With this defense, West would have been able to gain the lead and give me a diamond ruff.

Hand 14

A BLUFF PLAY

Most often, when you're playing cards and you're bluffing, you're playing poker. Once in a while, however, you can bluff when you're playing bridge.

Rubber bridge, neither side vulnerable.

Sitting East, I hold:

♠ K 8   ♡ A J 10 7 6 5   ♢ K Q 2   ♣ 8 3

I open the bidding with One Heart and South overcalls Two Diamonds. Partner raises to Two Hearts and North bids Three Diamonds.

On the auction, partner probably holds a singleton diamond. With the king-queen of diamonds opposite a singleton, I have a minimum hand. Nonetheless, I'm not going to sell out to Three Diamonds. I bid Three Hearts. South, however, leaps to Five Diamonds, which all Pass.

The Bidding:

NORTH	EAST	SOUTH	WEST
—	1 ♡	2 ♢	2 ♡
3 ♢	3 ♡	5 ♢	Pass
Pass	Pass		

Partner leads the king of hearts and North puts down this dummy:

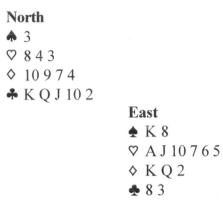

North
♠ 3
♡ 8 4 3
◇ 10 9 7 4
♣ K Q J 10 2

East
♠ K 8
♡ A J 10 7 6 5
◇ K Q 2
♣ 8 3

From the bidding, South should hold the ace of spades, a singleton heart, five or six diamonds ace-jack, and the ace of clubs. Partner cannot hold more than the king-queen of hearts and perhaps the queen of spades.

Playing Five Diamonds, declarer should lose only a heart and a diamond. I see a way, however, to present declarer with a guess. I overtake the king of hearts with the ace and return the three of clubs.

The complete hand:

North
♠ 3
♡ 8 4 3
◇ 10 9 7 4
♣ K Q J 10 2

West
♠ 10 9 7 6 5 4 2
♡ K Q 2
◇ —
♣ 7 6 5

East
♠ K 8
♡ A J 10 7 6 5
◇ K Q 2
♣ 8 3

South
♠ A Q J
♡ 9
◇ A J 8 6 5 3
♣ A 9 4

The low club is a bluff play. I don't have a singleton club. But declarer doesn't know that I can't ruff a club. Fearful of a club ruff, declarer wins the first club in dummy and leads a diamond to his ace, partner showing void. I later win the king and queen of diamonds, so Five Diamonds is down one.

If East plays a second heart at trick two, declarer should ruff and lead a low trump from hand. When West shows void in trumps, declarer knows to lead a club to dummy and then finesse the diamonds.

Hand 15

THE BANK OF OZ

A few months ago, I lent a friend of mine several hundred dollars. He promised to repay me within a week, but several months have passed and he still hasn't repaid me. I see him playing at another table. As soon as this hand is over, I'm going to ask him to repay the money he borrowed.

Meanwhile, partner and I bid to Four Spades on this auction.

The Bidding:

NORTH	EAST	SOUTH	WEST
Pass	Pass	1 ♠	Pass
2 ♠	Pass	4 ♠	Pass
Pass	Pass		

West leads the jack of hearts and North puts down this dummy:

North
♠ 9 4 3
♡ K Q 7
♢ 10 5 4 2
♣ K 7 3

South
♠ A K 7 6 2
♡ A 6 3
♢ A 8
♣ A 9 5

Four Spades is a good contract. If the spades break three-two, I can win ten tricks. But the spades may be breaking four-one. If so, it will be necessary to ruff two diamonds in hand.

I win the ace of hearts in hand and cash the ace of spades. I then lead a low diamond, which East wins with the jack. East returns the queen of spades to my king and West shows void, pitching a diamond.

I cash the ace of diamonds and East drops the king. From the play of the hand thus far, it appears that East holds the king-jack of diamonds doubleton. I must cash dummy's king and queen of hearts before ruffing a diamond, for I don't want East to pitch his last heart as I ruff a diamond. Fortunately, East follows as dummy wins the king and queen of hearts.

The rest of the hand is easy. I ruff a diamond to hand, East pitching a club. I continue with the ace and king of clubs and lead another diamond from dummy. East is unable to prevent me from making a small trump, so I make Four Spades.

The complete hand:

North
- ♠ 9 4 3
- ♥ K Q 7
- ♦ 10 5 4 2
- ♣ K 7 3

West
- ♠ 5
- ♥ J 10 9 4
- ♦ Q 9 7 6 3
- ♣ 10 8 6

East
- ♠ Q J 10 8
- ♥ 8 5 2
- ♦ K J
- ♣ Q J 4 2

South
- ♠ A K 7 6 2
- ♥ A 6 3
- ♦ A 8
- ♣ A 9 5

If declarer plays the ace and king of spades early, East will win a diamond and cash two spades. To make Four Spades, declarer must duck a diamond before playing a second round of spades. Later, declarer must cash three rounds of hearts before ruffing a diamond; otherwise, East pitches a heart on the third round of diamonds.

After the hand is over, I ask my friend to repay the money which he borrowed.

"I haven't got the money with me. But don't worry," he says, "the money is in the bank."

"What bank?" I ask.

"The Bank of Oz," he replies.

Hand 16

THE THIRD OPPONENT

Ordinarily, when you play rubber bridge, you have a partner and two opponents. Sometimes, however, your partner becomes a third opponent.

Sitting East, I hold:

♠ K Q J 10 9 6 4   ♡ —   ◊ Q J 7 2   ♣ J 10

South, on my left, opens the bidding with One Heart. Partner Passes and North, on my right, makes a limit raise of Three Hearts. I bid Four Spades, South bids Five Hearts and partner Doubles. All Pass, so the bidding has been:

NORTH	EAST	SOUTH	WEST
—	—	1 ♡	Pass
3 ♡	4 ♠	5 ♡	Dbl
Pass	Pass	Pass	

Partner leads the deuce of spades, an obvious singleton, and North puts down this dummy:

North
♠ 7 5 3
♡ A J 7
◊ K 6 5 3
♣ K 5 4

                                     East
                                     ♠ K Q J 10 9 6 4
                                     ♡ —
                                     ◊ Q J 7 2
                                     ♣ J 10

I play the nine of spades and South wins the ace. Declarer plays the king of hearts, a heart to dummy's jack and the ace of hearts. On the third heart partner drops the queen, declarer having started with seven hearts.

Declarer continues with a club to my ten which holds, South and West playing low. I play the king of spades, South follows, and partner pitches the ten of diamonds, undoubtedly showing the ace.

It's time now to count South's hand. South began with two spades and seven hearts. If South held a singleton diamond and three clubs, he would have led a diamond toward dummy's king. Declarer's failure to play a diamond toward dummy's king and his play of a low club to my ten virtually guarantee that South holds four clubs and is void in diamonds. South's hand must be:

♠ A x ♡ K x x x x x x ◊ - - ♣ A x x x

If I were to return either a spade or a diamond, South would ruff and then play his remaining trumps. This would be the position when South led his last trump:

North
♠ —
♡ —
◊ K x
♣ K x

West
♠ —
♡ —
◊ A
♣ Q x x

East
♠ —
♡ —
◊ Q J x
♣ J

South
♠ —
♡ x
◊ —
♣ A x x

The last trump would squeeze West in clubs and diamonds and declarer would make Five Hearts. To prevent this squeeze, I must return a club.

The complete hand:

North
♠ 7 5 3
♡ A J 7
◇ K 6 5 3
♣ K 5 4

West
♠ 2
♡ Q 10 6
◇ A 10 9 8 4
♣ Q 9 6 3

East
♠ K Q J 10 9 6 4
♡ —
◇ Q J 7 2
♣ J 10

South
♠ A 8
♡ K 9 8 5 4 3 2
◇ —
♣ A 8 7 2

This hand has a happy ending for my opponents. Declarer wins the king of clubs in dummy, ruffs a spade to hand and leads all his remaining trumps. I pitch the queen and deuce of diamonds, to show four diamonds. Nonetheless, partner pitches a club on the last trump, saving the ace of diamonds, so declarer makes Five Hearts, Doubled.

Partner is critical of my defense. "If you had returned a diamond as I asked," said West, "I would have discovered that declarer was void of diamonds and saved the clubs. It's your fault declarer made Five Hearts."

"You're right," I concede, "I should have returned a diamond rather than a club."

The truth is that with this particular partner, I misdefended the hand. After winning the ten of clubs, I should have returned a club right away, without first cashing a high spade. Partner would then have been able to hold both the ace of diamonds and the clubs. And if declarer later led a spade, I could win the spade and return a diamond.

Hand 17

AVERTING AN OVERRUFF

Playing rubber bridge, partner and I bid to Four Spades on the following auction:

NORTH	EAST	SOUTH	WEST
—	—	—	1 ♥
Dbl	2 ♥	3 ♠	4 ♥
4 ♠	Pass	Pass	Pass

West leads the king of hearts and North puts down this dummy:

North
♠ J 7 5
♥ Q 3
♦ A Q 10 3
♣ A K 4 2

South
♠ K Q 10 6 4
♥ 7
♦ K 9 4 2
♣ 8 7 5

West wins the king of hearts and continues with the ace of hearts. Dummy plays the queen of hearts, East a low heart, and I discard a club. A club discard is best because a club must be lost in any event. If I were to ruff the second heart, I would lose control if the trumps divide four-one.

West shifts to the seven of diamonds, which may be a singleton. To insure a later entry to hand I cover with dummy's ten, East plays the jack of diamonds and I win with the king. I lead a spade to dummy's jack, which holds, and continue with a spade to my ten. East shows void on the second spade, pitching a heart, and West ducks the second spade.

It looks correct now to play a third spade, for I must draw West's last trump before running the diamonds. But I see some danger in playing a third trump. If West wins the ace of spades and plays a club, I would be stuck in dummy. I would then be forced to exit dummy by leading a diamond, which West might ruff, or by playing the ace and king of clubs and ruffing a club, which West might overruff.

To avert being trapped in dummy and exposed to an overruff in clubs, I play the ace and king of clubs before leading a third round of spades. West wins the third round of spades, but no matter how West continues, I will be able to return to hand and draw his last trump, making Four Spades.

The complete hand:

```
                    North
                    ♠ J 7 5
                    ♡ Q 3
                    ◊ A Q 10 3
                    ♣ A K 4 2
     West                               East
     ♠ A 9 8 2                          ♠ 3
     ♡ A K 9 8 6 4                      ♡ J 10 5 2
     ◊ 7                                ◊ J 8 6 5
     ♣ 10 9                             ♣ Q J 6 3
                    South
                    ♠ K Q 10 6 4
                    ♡ 7
                    ◊ K 9 4 2
                    ♣ 8 7 5
```

This hand has several interesting points. If declarer ruffs the second heart, instead of pitching a club, he loses control when the spades divide four-one.

If North plays low on the first lead of diamonds, rather than the ten, East plays the jack and South wins the king. Later, after West wins the third round of spades, West may be able to lead a second diamond, putting North on play. If West leads a second diamond, which is won in dummy, declarer will then be unable to return to hand without exposing himself to an overruff in clubs.

If declarer fails to play the ace and king of clubs before leading a third round of spades, West can win the third spade and lead a club. West then makes the nine of spades by overruffing the third round of clubs.

Hand 18

A MATCH-POINT ADVENTURE

Playing duplicate bridge, with North-South vulnerable, I hold the following hand as South:

♠ A   ♡ A K 7 6 4 2   ◊ 8 7 5 4   ♣ K 7

I open the bidding with One Heart. West bids Three Spades, partner bids Four Hearts, and East bids Four Spades. We can probably set Four Spades two tricks, for a penalty of 300 points. But this would be a poor match-point score. I therefore bid Five Hearts, which should have a good chance of making, and all Pass.

The Bidding:

NORTH	EAST	SOUTH	WEST
—	—	1 ♡	3 ♠
4 ♡	4 ♠	5 ♡	Pass
Pass	Pass	Pass	

West leads the king of spades and North puts down this dummy:

North
♠ 8 3
♡ Q J 10 3
◊ K 6 2
♣ A Q 9 4

South
♠ A
♡ A K 7 6 4 2
◊ 8 7 5 4
♣ K 7

I have ten top tricks consisting of a spade, six hearts, and three clubs. At first sight, Five Hearts appears to depend upon West holding the ace of diamonds.

But East is almost certain to hold the ace of diamonds. If I were to lead a diamond to dummy's king, I would lose three tricks in diamonds and Five Hearts would be down one. But if East holds four or more clubs, I can make Five Hearts on an endplay.

I win the ace of spades, play the ace and queen of hearts, and ruff a spade. I continue with the king, ace, and queen of clubs, pitching a diamond, as all follow. This is the position when I lead dummy's last club.

North
♠ —
♡ J 10
♢ K 6 2
♣ 9

West
♠ Q J 10 9
♡ —
♢ 10 3
♣ —

East
♠ 6
♡ —
♢ A Q J 9
♣ J

South
♠ —
♡ K 7 6
♢ 8 7 5
♣ —

I lead dummy's nine of clubs, East plays the jack, and I pitch another diamond. This endplays East. A spade return will allow me to sluff a diamond from hand and ruff in dummy, while a diamond return will be from East's ace-queen into dummy's king. I make Five Hearts, for a good match-point score.

The complete hand:

North
♠ 8 3
♡ Q J 10 3
◊ K 6 2
♣ A Q 9 4

West
♠ K Q J 10 9 7 2
♡ 9
◊ 10 3
♣ 6 3 2

East
♠ 6 5 4
♡ 8 5
◊ A Q J 9
♣ J 10 8 5

South
♠ A
♡ A K 7 6 4 2
◊ 8 7 5 4
♣ K 7

At duplicate bridge, you frequently see non-vulnerable defenders taking a save against a vulnerable game. The vulnerable pair must then decide whether to double and accept a small penalty, or bid on and possibly be set.

On this hand if North-South Doubles Four Spades, they obtain a penalty of 300 points and a below average match-point score. North-South therefore take the push to Five Hearts which yields 650 points and an above average match-point score. But if West guesses to lead a diamond, Five Hearts goes down one.

Hand 19

TEST YOUR BIDDING

This hand comes from a rubber bridge game. Partner and I are playing five card majors and strong jump shifts. Sitting South, I hold:

♠ K 6 5 3   ♡ 7   ◇ A K Q 9 7 3   ♣ K 2

Partner, sitting North, opens the bidding with One Spade and I jump to Three Diamonds. North rebids Three Hearts and I bid Three Spades. Partner bids Four Spades and I must now consider whether or not to bid a slam.

Partner's failure to bid Four Clubs over my Three Spade bid suggests that he has a minimum hand without the ace of clubs. Nonetheless, if partner holds the ace-queen of spades and the ace of hearts, we should have a good play for Six Spades. I bid Four No-Trump, Blackwood, and partner responds Five Hearts, showing two aces.

It appears that I should bid Six Spades, rather than Six Diamonds, for we have a five-four spade fit. But before making my next bid, I'm going to give some consideration to several possible hands which partner might hold on the auction. Partner appears to have five spades and four hearts. His remaining cards are likely to be two diamonds and two clubs or a singleton diamond and three clubs. Partner probably holds one of the following hands:

1. ♠ A Q J x x   ♡ A J x x   ◇ x   ♣ Q x x

2. ♠ A Q x x x   ♡ A Q x x   ◇ x x   ♣ x x

3. ♠ A x x x x   ♡ A K J x   ◇ x   ♣ x x x

4. ♠ A x x x x   ♡ A K J x   ◇ x x   ♣ x x

On the first hand, with North holding good spades and the queen of clubs, Six Spades is the best contract. On the second hand, with North holding good spades, a doubleton diamond, and nothing in clubs, Six Diamonds is the best contract because the king of clubs is protected.

On the third hand, with North holding weak spades, a singleton diamond, and nothing in clubs, Four Spades is the best contract. On the fourth hand, with North holding weak spades, a doubleton diamond, and nothing in clubs, Six Diamonds is the best contract.

After considering the possibilities for several seconds, I bid Six Diamonds. Partner knows that I have spade support for him and he should bid Six Spades if he holds a singleton diamond. Partner passes, however, so Six Diamonds becomes the final contract.

The complete hand:

North
♠ A 10 8 4 2
♡ A K Q 3
◊ J 2
♣ 7 4

West
♠ 9
♡ J 9 8 6 4
◊ 10 8
♣ A 10 8 6 5

East
♠ Q J 7
♡ 10 5 2
◊ 6 5 4
♣ Q J 9 3

South
♠ K 6 5 3
♡ 7
◊ A K Q 9 7 3
♣ K 2

As it turns out, partner holds the perfect hand for me and Six Diamonds cannot be set. Six Spades, on the other hand, goes down two with East leading the queen of clubs.

Most players, holding four spades to an honor and aware that North holds five spades, would automatically bid Six Spades with the South hand. But if you think of the many hands which North might hold on the auction, you should realize that Six Diamonds may be a better contract than Six Spades.

Hand 20

THE ROAD TO SUCCESS

The road to success in the play of a bridge hand is a three step process. First, you must consider the likely distribution of the opponents' hands. Second, you must consider which of your opponents is likely to hold the missing high cards. And third, you must then adopt a line of play which has the best chance to succeed against the hands which your opponents are likely to hold.

Join me now, dear reader, as I follow this three step process while playing Four Spades.

The Bidding:

NORTH	EAST	SOUTH	WEST
—	1 ◊	1 ♠	Pass
3 ◊**	Pass	4 ♠	Pass
Pass	Pass	Pass	Pass

**Strong limit raise

North
- ♠ Q 10 9 7
- ♡ K 4 3
- ◊ K 6
- ♣ K 10 4 2

South
- ♠ A K J 8 5
- ♡ A J 6
- ◊ J 8 4
- ♣ Q 5

West leads the ten of diamonds. East wins the queen and ace of diamonds and leads a third diamond to my jack. West ruffs low and dummy overruffs with the seven.

Four Spades is almost sure to make. I have eight top tricks outside of clubs, consisting of five spades, two hearts, and a diamond ruff in dummy. I can make Four Spades if I win two tricks in clubs or the heart finesse works.

East, who opened the bidding, must hold the ace of clubs. I can win two tricks in clubs if East holds the ace of clubs doubleton or third, by leading a club to my queen, and later ruffing out East's ace of clubs. I can also win a second club trick by finessing the ten of clubs, which will succeed if West holds the jack of clubs.

I begin by cashing the ace of spades and leading a spade to dummy's ten. West discards a heart on the second spade. East follows, having started with two spades. I then lead a low club from dummy to my queen, which holds.

It looks correct now to continue with a club to dummy's ten. But is this the best play?

East began with two spades and six diamonds ace-queen. East's remaining cards ought to be three hearts and two clubs, two hearts and three clubs, or possibly, one heart and four clubs. East should hold one of the following hands:

1. ♠ x x ♡ x x x ♢ A Q 9 x x x ♣ A x

2. ♠ x x ♡ x x ♢ A Q 9 x x x ♣ A x x

3. ♠ x x ♡ x x ♢ A Q 9 x x x ♣ A J x

4. ♠ x x ♡ x ♢ A Q 9 x x x ♣ A x x x

5. ♠ x x ♡ x ♢ A Q 9 x x x ♣ A J 9 x

On the first hand, it doesn't matter that the club finesse works, for the ace of clubs is doubleton. On the second and third hands, it doesn't matter whether or not the club finesse works, for the ace of clubs ruffs out in any event. On the fourth hand, I can make Four Spades by finessing dummy's ten of clubs.

But on the fifth hand, the club finesse loses and the ace of clubs fails to ruff out. If I were to lead a club to dummy's ten now, East would win the jack of clubs and exit with a heart and Four Spades would be down one.

That is why I must cash the ace of hearts before taking the club finesse.

The complete hand:

North
- ♠ Q 10 9 7
- ♡ K 4 3
- ♢ K 6
- ♣ K 10 4 2

West
- ♠ 3 2
- ♡ Q 10 9 7 5 2
- ♢ 10 2
- ♣ 8 7 3

East
- ♠ 6 4
- ♡ 8
- ♢ A Q 9 7 5 3
- ♣ A J 9 6

South
- ♠ A K J 8 5
- ♡ A J 6
- ♢ J 8 4
- ♣ Q 5

Cashing the ace of hearts before taking the club finesse prevents East from exiting with a heart. After winning the jack of clubs, East is forced to play either a diamond, which gives me a sluff and a ruff, or a club from his ace, so I make Four Spades.

Hand 21

AN UNUSUAL MEAL

After playing Chinese Poker for $10 a point and losing $500, I decide to play a few hours of rubber bridge.

Sitting South, I hold:

♠ K Q 9   ♡ A Q 9 2   ◊ Q 9   ♣ A Q 9 7

Just my bad luck with this hand that I'm playing rubber bridge instead of Chinese Poker. At Chinese Poker, I could play A-A-K in the front hand, four nines in the middle hand and four queens in the back hand. At $10 per point, with bonuses for quads, sweeps, and a "home run", this hand would be worth more than the $500 I lost earlier.

Oh well, at least it's rubber bridge instead of duplicate. I should be able to win back some of the $500 which I lost earlier.

I open the bidding with One Club. West, on my left, Passes and partner responds One Diamond. East Passes. I rebid Two No-Trump and partner raises me to Three No-Trump, which all Pass.

The Bidding:

NORTH	EAST	SOUTH	WEST
—	—	1 ♣	Pass
1 ◊	Pass	2NT	Pass
3NT	Pass	Pass	Pass

North
♠ 5
♡ K J 5
◇ A J 10 8 3 2
♣ 10 8 6

South
♠ K Q 9
♡ A Q 9 2
◇ Q 9
♣ A Q 9 7

West leads the seven of spades, dummy plays low, East the ten, and I win the queen. From the play thus far, it appears that West holds five or six spades to the ace-jack.

The normal play is to finesse the queen of diamonds. If West holds the king of diamonds, I should be able to win six diamonds, four hearts, a spade and a club, for a total of twelve tricks. But if the diamond finesse loses, East will win the king of diamonds and return a spade, setting Three No-Trump.

At rubber bridge, the focus is upon making your contract, not on making overtricks. If I play the clubs instead of taking the diamond finesse, I can make Three No-Trump if East holds either the king or the jack of clubs. By playing clubs instead of diamonds, I can make Three No-Trump 75% of the time instead of the mere 50% chance which the diamond finesse provides.

I lead a heart to dummy's jack and continue with the eight of clubs from dummy, which West wins with the jack. West defends well by shifting to a diamond. I win dummy's ace of diamonds, and lead dummy's ten of clubs for a second club finesse.

Unfortunately, West wins the king of clubs. West leads a second diamond to East's king. East returns a spade through my king and West runs the spade suit. West holds six spades, rather than five, so Three No-Trump is down four.

West congratulates himself for his fine defense in shifting to a diamond. West then comments that perhaps he should have doubled Three No-Trump and collected 1100 points instead of a measly 400 points. Meanwhile, partner and I suffer while West gloats.

The complete hand:

North
♠ 5
♡ K J 5
◊ A J 10 8 3 2
♣ 10 8 6

West
♠ A J 8 7 4 2
♡ 10 7
◊ 7 4
♣ K J 2

East
♠ 10 6 3
♡ 8 6 4 3
◊ K 6 5
♣ 5 4 3

South
♠ K Q 9
♡ A Q 9 2
◊ Q 9
♣ A Q 9 7

Some days, no matter how well you play, you can't win. This is one of those days. I pay my losses, go home and turn on the television set for the latest news in stocks. I learn that one of my stocks, Micron Technology, has announced an earnings shortfall and fallen four points. This results in a $4,000 loss for me, which dwarfs my losses at Chinese Poker and bridge. Guess I'll eat some worms.

Hand 22

THE SHAGGY DOG

My left hand opponent is totally bald. His head looks like a billiard ball. Partner, on the other hand, has hair that extends several inches lower than his shoulders. He looks like a shaggy dog. They have one thing in common. Neither of them ever visits a barber.

Sitting West, I hold:

♠ J 5 4 2   ♡ 2   ◊ Q 9 7 6   ♣ K J 8 3

Partner, sitting East, opens the bidding with One Heart. South, at my right, overcalls Four Spades. I Double and North passes. Partner, however, pulls my double and bids Five Diamonds. South Passes, I Pass, and North bids Five Spades. Partner Passes, South Passes, and I Double again. This time, all Pass.

The Bidding:

NORTH	EAST	SOUTH	WEST
—	1 ♡	4 ♠	Dbl
Pass	5 ◊	Pass	Pass
5 ♠	Pass	Pass	Dbl
Pass	Pass	Pass	

I lead the deuce of hearts and North puts down this dummy:

North
♠ Q 8
♡ K Q 10 7 5
◊ 8 5 3 2
♣ A 7

West
♠ J 5 4 2
♡ 2
◊ Q 9 7 6
♣ K J 8 3

Partner wins the ace of hearts, South playing the three. Partner returns the nine of hearts, South the jack, and I ruff. Partner's nine of hearts is a clear suit preference for diamonds. Before leading a diamond, however, I'm going to give some thought to the likely lie of the cards.

South almost certainly holds seven spades for his Four Spade bid, which means East is void in spades. Since East bid five diamonds over my Double, rather than Four No-Trump for the minors, East undoubtedly holds five diamonds and South must be void in diamonds. East's hand ought to be either:

1. ♠ — ♡ A x x x x   ◊ A K J x x   ♣ x x x

2. ♠ — ♡ A x x x x   ◊ A K J x x   ♣ Q x x

South's hand ought to be either:

1. ♠ A K x x x x x ♡ J x ◊ — ♣ Q x x x

2. ♠ A K x x x x x ♡ J x ◊ — ♣ x x x x

I can see what will happen if I play a diamond. South will ruff, pull trumps, enter dummy with the ace of clubs and pitch three clubs on dummy's hearts, making Five Spades Doubled.

The ace of clubs is the entry to the hearts. Instead of leading a diamond, I must lead a club, to knock out dummy's ace. Since partner may not hold the queen of clubs, I play the king of clubs, which declarer wins with dummy's ace.

At this point, declarer could continue with a club to his queen and ruff two clubs in dummy, but then my jack of spades would promote to the setting trick. In practice, declarer plays the ace of spades and a spade to dummy's queen. Declarer then finesses the ten of clubs, which I win with the jack, so Five Spades goes down one, Doubled.

The complete hand:

North
♠ Q 8
♡ K Q 10 7 5
◇ 8 5 3 2
♣ A 7

West
♠ J 5 4 2
♡ 2
◇ Q 9 7 6
♣ K J 8 3

East
♠ —
♡ A 9 8 6 4
◇ A K J 10 4
♣ 5 4 2

South
♠ A K 10 9 7 6 3
♡ J 3
◇ —
♣ Q 10 9 6

Declarer can make Five Spades if he guesses to play the queen of clubs and run the ten through West. But if East had held the queen, ten or nine of clubs, Five Spades would always be set.

After the session ends, I find myself several hundred dollars richer. I offer to treat the Shaggy Dog to a hair cut. "No thanks," he says, "I like my hair long."

I saw him again a few weeks later. I noticed that his hair was much better kept. He had placed a rubber band around it, creating a pig tail for himself.

Hand 23

TWO UNUSUAL PLAYS

On this hand West must make two unusual plays to set Four Hearts.

Playing rubber bridge, I hold:

♠ K Q J 4   ♡ A 9 8 3   ♦ J 10 2   ♣ A 4

Sitting West, I open the bidding with One No-Trump. North and East Pass and South, at my right, Doubles. I Pass and North, at my left, bids Two Clubs. Partner Passes and South bids Three Hearts. I Pass and North bids Four Hearts, which all Pass.

The Bidding:

NORTH	EAST	SOUTH	WEST
—	—	—	1NT
Pass	Pass	Dbl	Pass
2 ♣	Pass	3 ♡	Pass
4 ♡	Pass	Pass	Pass

I lead the king of spades and North puts down this dummy:

North
♠ 9 7 3
♡ 5
♦ A Q 6 4
♣ Q 10 9 8 5

West
♠ K Q J 4
♡ A 9 8 3
♦ J 10 2
♣ A 4

Declarer wins the king of spades with the ace, partner playing low. Declarer continues with the king of diamonds, ace of diamonds and queen of diamonds, pitching a club. Declarer persists with a fourth round of diamonds, partner plays the nine, declarer pitches a second club and it is my play. Before discarding on the fourth round of diamonds, I stop to consider South's hand.

Declarer began with two diamonds and two clubs. Declarer's remaining cards ought to be seven hearts and the doubleton ace of spades. Declarer's hand should be:

♠ A-x   ♡ K-Q-J-10-x-x-x   ◊ K-x   ♣ x-x

It appears that the defense will win a diamond, a spade and a heart. In order to set Four Hearts, it will be necessary to win two trump tricks.

South's two club discards show that he does not hold the king of clubs. It must be correct, therefore, to pitch the ace of clubs! This play is necessary in order to promote the nine of hearts into the setting trick.

Partner does his part by playing the king of clubs, which declarer ruffs. If declarer had pitched a spade on the king of clubs, then another club from partner would set four hearts.

Declarer plays the king of hearts, which I duck, and the queen of hearts, which I win with the ace. Partner shows void on the second heart, declarer having started with seven hearts. Declarer's distribution is in fact 7-2-2-2.

It's necessary now to underlead the queen-jack of spades. Fortunately, partner is able to win the trick with the ten of spades. Partner returns a club, which promotes my nine of hearts, so we set Four Spades one trick.

The complete hand:

North
♠ 9 7 3
♡ 5
♢ A Q 6 4
♣ Q 10 9 8 5

West
♠ K Q J 4
♡ A 9 8 3
♢ J 10 2
♣ A 4

East
♠ 10 8 6 2
♡ 4
♢ 9 7 5 3
♣ K J 6 2

South
♠ A 5
♡ K Q J 10 7 6 2
♢ K 8
♣ 7 3

If declarer leads a trump after cashing three rounds of diamonds, the defense still prevails. West wins the ace of hearts, cashes a spade, and underleads his ace of clubs to East's king-jack. East then plays a diamond, which promotes the nine of hearts for West.

Hand 24

A LATE BREAKFAST

Due to an early morning court appearance, I skip breakfast. After court, I go to the Cavendish West Club in Los Angeles for an afternoon of bridge.

Sitting South, I hold:

♠ A 8 3   ♡ A K Q J 6 4   ◊ 7   ♣ A 5 4

I open the bidding with Two Clubs, strong and artificial. West passes and partner responds Two Diamonds, showing less than eight high card points. East, on my right, bids Three Spades. I bid Four Hearts, West Passes, and partner raises me to Five Hearts. East Passes and I bid Six Hearts, which all Pass.

The Bidding:

NORTH	EAST	SOUTH	WEST
—	—	2 ♣	Pass
2 ◊	3 ♠	4 ♡	Pass
5 ♡	Pass	6 ♡	Pass
Pass	Pass		

West leads the seven of spades and North puts down this dummy:

North
♠ 9
♡ 7 5 2
◊ A 8 6 4 3
♣ K 8 6 2

South
♠ A 8 3
♡ A K Q J 6 4
◊ 7
♣ A 5 4

I have ten top tricks. Ordinarily, I'd play to ruff two spades in dummy to bring the total to twelve tricks. But East is likely to hold seven spades for his Three Spade bid, so I won't be able to ruff two spades in dummy. Therefore, I plan to ruff only one spade in dummy. I should be able to win a twelfth trick either with a squeeze against West in the minors or a double squeeze.

I win the ace of spades and duck a club. East wins the club and continues with a high spade which I ruff in dummy. I play three rounds of trump, West following to all three, East showing void after the first round. I continue with the king and ace of clubs. On the third club East shows void, West having started with four clubs. I then lead out all of my remaining trumps.

This is the position when I lead my last trump:

North
♠
♡
♢ A 8
♣ 6

West
♠
♡
♢ K 10
♣ Q

East
♠ K
♡
♢ Q J
♣

South
♠ 8
♡ K
♢ 7
♣

On the last trump West is forced to discard a diamond to protect the queen of clubs. I discard dummy's club and now it is East who is squeezed. East discards a diamond in order to hold the king of spades, so dummy's ace and eight of diamonds win the last two tricks.

The complete hand:

North
♠ 9
♡ 7 5 2
♢ A 8 6 4 3
♣ K 8 6 2

West
♠ 7 5
♡ 10 9 3
♢ K 10 9 2
♣ Q 10 7 3

East
♠ K Q J 10 6 4 2
♡ 8
♢ Q J 5
♣ J 9

South
♠ A 8 3
♡ A K Q J 6 4
♢ 7
♣ A 5 4

If East returns a diamond after winning the club, then declarer wins the ace of diamonds, ruffs a diamond, ruffs a spade in dummy, and ruffs another diamond to establish a threat against West. On the run of the hearts West is squeezed in the minors.

After the hand is over I order steak and eggs, telling the waitress that I was having a late breakfast. "Kauder," says West, "I can see you haven't eaten today. You're not wearing any food."

Hand 25

DISRUPTING COMMUNICATIONS

Playing rubber bridge, I hold:

♠ 10 9 8 2   ♡ A K Q 7   ◊ K J 10   ♣ 10 4

South, on my left, opens the bidding with One Club and partner passes. North, on my right, responds One Diamond and I Double. South rebids One Spade, partner Passes and North bids Four Spades, which all Pass.

The Bidding:

NORTH	EAST	SOUTH	WEST
—	—	1 ♣	Pass
1 ◊	Dbl	1 ♠	Pass
4 ♠	Pass	Pass	Pass

Partner leads a low heart and North puts down this dummy:

North
♠ A J 7 5
♡ J 5 2
◊ A Q 3 2
♣ Q 6

East
♠ 10 9 8 2
♡ A K Q 7
◊ K J 10
♣ 10 4

I win the queen and king of hearts and continue with a third heart, which declarer ruffs. Declarer plays the king of spades and all follow. Declarer next plays a diamond to dummy's queen and my king.

Four Spades can never be made if declarer holds three diamonds. I need worry only if declarer began with a doubleton diamond. If so, South's hand would consist of four spades, two hearts, two diamonds and five clubs. South's hand would then be:

♠ K Q x x   ♡ x x   ◇ x x   ♣ A K x x x

It looks natural to return the jack of diamonds to dummy's ace. But if South began with a doubleton diamond, he will win the ace of diamonds in dummy, ruff a diamond to hand, cash the queen of spades, lead a club to dummy's queen and cash the ace and jack of spades. Declarer will then come to ten tricks via four spades, a heart ruff, the ace of diamonds and a diamond ruff, and the ace, king and queen of clubs.

A spade, heart or a diamond return will allow declarer to make Four Spades. That is why I must return a club. The club return foils declarer's plans by removing the entry to dummy's trumps before declarer can ruff a diamond.

Declarer wins the queen of clubs in dummy and then plays the ace of diamonds and ruffs a diamond. Declarer next plays the queen of spades, partner showing void.

If partner had followed to the queen of spades, declarer would have been able to overtake the queen of spades and pull the remaining trumps. But with West showing void on the second spade, declarer is forced to play a low spade under his queen.

Declarer continues with the ace and king of clubs, pitching dummy's losing diamond. But I ruff the king of clubs, so Four Spades is down one.

The complete hand:

North
- ♠ A J 7 5
- ♡ J 5 2
- ◊ A Q 3 2
- ♣ Q 6

West
- ♠ 3
- ♡ 10 8 4 3
- ◊ 9 8 7 4
- ♣ J 9 7 5

East
- ♠ 10 9 8 2
- ♡ A K Q 7
- ◊ K J 10
- ♣ 10 4

South
- ♠ K Q 6 4
- ♡ 9 6
- ◊ 6 5
- ♣ A K 8 3 2

Hand 26

THE ART STUDENT

In order to get a degree in mathematics, I was required to take a course in music or art. I chose a beginning art course. I was the worst student in the class. No matter how much effort I put into studying art, I could not master the subject. I barely passed. Too bad my college didn't offer a bridge course instead. It would have been easy for me.

Sitting East, I hold:

♠ 8 6   ♡ A K Q 8 7   ◇ K 6 5   ♣ K J 2

I open the bidding with One Heart. South, on my left, overcalls One Spade. Partner passes and North, on my right, bids Four Spades, which all Pass.

The bidding has been:

NORTH	EAST	SOUTH	WEST
—	1 ♡	1 ♠	Pass
4 ♠	Pass	Pass	Pass

Partner leads the deuce of hearts and North puts down this dummy:

North
♠ 9 7 4 3
♡ J 4 3
◇ A 7
♣ A Q 10 9

East
♠ 8 6
♡ A K Q 8 7
◇ K 6 5
♣ K J 2

I win the queen and king of hearts and continue with the ace of hearts, which declarer ruffs. Declarer plays the ace and king of spades and partner drops the queen. Declarer then leads a club to dummy's queen, which I win with the king.

I must now decide the best return. A heart return will give declarer a sluff and a ruff. A diamond return from my king is likely to give up a trick. And a club lead from my jack into dummy's ace-ten-nine is also likely to give up a trick. Woe is me.

In order to determine the best defense, I count declarer's hand. South began with five spades and two hearts. South's other six cards ought to be two diamonds and four clubs, three diamonds and three clubs or four diamonds and two clubs. South should hold one of the following hands:

1. ♠ A K J 10 x   ♡ x x   ◇ Q x   ♣ x x x x

2. ♠ A K J 10 x   ♡ x x   ◇ Q J x   ♣ x x x

3. ♠ A K J 10 x   ♡ x x   ◇ Q J x x   ♣ x x

On the first hand, it doesn't matter how I defend. A heart, a diamond or a club return will set declarer.

On the second hand, a diamond return will leave declarer with a losing club and a club return will leave declarer with a losing diamond. And even with a heart return, declarer must still lose a club or a diamond. If declarer holds the second hand, Four Spades will always be set.

If declarer holds the third hand, however, a diamond return will allow declarer to win the queen and ace of diamonds and then ruff out my jack of clubs. And a heart return would allow declarer to ruff in hand and pitch a diamond from dummy. Declarer could then play the ace of clubs and ruff out my jack of clubs, making Four Spades.

But a club return, from my jack into dummy's ace-ten-nine, will set Four Spades no matter what hand declarer holds. To be sure of setting Four Spades, I return a club from my jack into dummy's ace-ten-nine.

The complete hand:

North
- ♠ 9 7 4 3
- ♡ J 4 3
- ◇ A 7
- ♣ A Q 10 9

West
- ♠ Q 2
- ♡ 10 6 2
- ◇ 10 8 4 2
- ♣ 8 7 4 3

East
- ♠ 8 6
- ♡ A K Q 8 7
- ◇ K 6 5
- ♣ K J 2

South
- ♠ A K J 10 5
- ♡ 9 5
- ◇ Q J 9 3
- ♣ 6 5

Earlier, I made a slight error in defense. After winning the queen and king of hearts, I should have shifted to a trump. Declarer would play the ace and king of spades and then take the club finesse. After winning the king of clubs, it would not have been necessary for me to return a club into dummy's ace-ten-nine. I would have been able to play the ace of hearts.

So what did my story about a college art course have to do with bridge? Nothing at all. Just a suggestion, dear reader. Everyone has some skills and some weak points. You should focus your energy upon the areas in which you have natural abilities, for there lies the road to both satisfaction and success.

Hand 27

BRIDE AND GROOM

My partner this rubber is an old friend whom I haven't seen in several years. He tells me that he was recently married. That's nice. I look forward to meeting his wife.

Sitting West, I hold:

♠ 7 5   ♡ A K Q 10 2   ◊ A 10 6   ♣ 9 7 3

South, at my right, opens the bidding with One Spade and I overcall Two Hearts. North leaps to Four Spades, which all Pass.

The Bidding:

NORTH	EAST	SOUTH	WEST
—	—	1 ♠	2 ♡
4 ♠	Pass	Pass	Pass

I lead the king of hearts and North puts down this dummy:

North
♠ Q J 9 6
♡ 5
◊ 8 7 5
♣ A Q J 8 4

West
♠ 7 5
♡ A K Q 10 2
◊ A 10 6
♣ 9 7 3

The king of hearts wins, partner playing the nine to show four. From the auction, it's likely that South holds five spades ace-king and three hearts. Declarer's remaining cards ought to be three diamonds and two clubs or two diamonds and three clubs.

To set Four Spades, it will be necessary for the defense to win three tricks in diamonds and clubs. If declarer holds the king of clubs, I must shift to a low diamond. Then if partner holds the king-queen of diamonds or the king-jack of diamonds, we can set Four Spades.

A low diamond will also set Four Spades when partner holds the king of clubs and either the queen or jack of diamonds. After winning the king of clubs, partner will return a diamond to my ace-ten and the defense will win two diamond tricks.

A low diamond sets Four Spades when declarer holds any of the following hands:

1. ♠ A K x x x   ♡ J x x   ◊ K Q x   ♣ x x

2. ♠ A K x x x   ♡ J x x   ◊ Q x x   ♣ K x

3. ♠ A K x x x   ♡ J x x   ◊ J x x   ♣ K x

On the other hand, a diamond shift would allow declarer to make Four Spades if he held:

4. ♠ A K x x x   ♡ J x x   ◊ K x   ♣ x x x

It appears more likely that South will hold one of the first three hands rather than the fourth. On the fourth hand, South holds only eleven high card points and he probably would not have opened the bidding. I therefore shift to a low diamond.

Partner plays the jack of diamonds and declarer wins the queen. Declarer plays two rounds of spades and then tries the club finesse, partner winning the king. East returns a diamond to my ace-ten, so Four Spades is down one.

The complete hand:

North
♠ Q J 9 6
♡ 5
◊ 8 7 5
♣ A Q J 8 4

West
♠ 7 5
♡ A K Q 10 2
◊ A 10 6
♣ 9 7 3

East
♠ 4 2
♡ 9 8 6 3
◊ J 9 3 2
♣ K 5 2

South
♠ A K 10 8 3
♡ J 7 4
◊ K Q 4
♣ 10 6

After the session was over, my friend shows me a picture of his wife. She was very pretty. I congratulate my friend on his good fortune. No doubt about it. She'll make him a nice first wife.

Hand 28

TO TELL THE TRUTH

Unlike most poker players, and some attorneys, I'm willing to tell the truth about myself. After playing poker several times a week for many years, I've come to the conclusion that I have limited skills at poker. In fact, I'm a regular donator at the poker tables.

That is why I prefer playing bridge. At bridge, I've got far greater than average skills. And if I play often, I usually win enough to cover my poker losses.

Playing rubber bridge, with neither side vulnerable, I hold the following hand as West:

♠ J 5 4   ♡ K Q 10 8 4   ◇ A K Q   ♣ K Q

North, on my left, opens the bidding with One Club. Partner, sitting East, Passes. South, on my right, bids One Spade and I bid Two Hearts. North leaps to Four Spades, East and South Pass, and it is my bid.

North's Four Spade bid is undoubtedly based upon distribution, not high cards. North may well hold five clubs and five spades, in which case Four Spades may be cold.

On the auction, it's likely that partner holds a singleton spade. If partner holds as little as five diamonds to the jack or four hearts to the jack, we should have a good save against Four Spades. At Five Diamonds or Five Hearts, it's likely we will lose only three tricks; the ace of clubs, the ace of hearts, and a spade.

With twenty high card points, I'm not about to Pass, so I Double Four Spades. Partner should be able to determine whether to bid on or defend. All Pass, so Four Spades Doubled becomes the final contract.

The Bidding:

NORTH	EAST	SOUTH	WEST
1 ♣	Pass	1 ♠	2 ♡
4 ♠	Pass	Pass	Dbl
Pass	Pass	Pass	

I lead the king of diamonds and North puts down this dummy:

North
♠ A K Q 8
♡ 5
◊ 7 5
♣ A 8 7 6 4 3

West
♠ J 5 4
♡ K Q 10 8 4
◊ A K Q
♣ K Q

The king of diamonds holds, partner playing the four. I continue with the queen of diamonds which holds, partner playing the six. Partner's play in diamonds shows either three or five. Given the bidding, I'm going to assume that partner holds five diamonds rather than three.

It must be right to make dummy ruff a diamond now, before declarer can start the clubs, so I continue with the ace of diamonds which is ruffed low in dummy, declarer playing the jack.

Declarer plays the ace of clubs and ruffs a club to hand, partner having started with the J-10-9-5 of clubs. Declarer continues with a spade to dummy's queen and ruffs another club with the ten of spades.

At first sight, it looks correct to overruff the club with the jack of spades. But before overruffing, I'm going to give some thought to South's distribution and the likely play of the hand.

South began with a singleton club. Since he bid One Spade over North's one club opener, rather than bid One Diamond or One Heart, South ought to have a five card spade suit. South's hand should be:

♠ 10-9-8-x-x   ♡ A-J-x-x   ◊ J-x-x   ♣ x

I can see what will happen if I overruff the club. Declarer will win the king of hearts return in hand with the ace, lead a trump to dummy, and ruff another club. North's hand, consisting of the last trump and two more clubs, would then be high and North-South would make Four Spades Doubled.

On the other hand, by not overruffing, I should be able to set Four Spades. Declarer will be able to set up the clubs, but he won't be able to get to dummy's clubs without ruffing a heart with dummy's last trump. Instead of overruffing, I pitch a heart on the third round of clubs.

Declarer continues with a trump to dummy's king, partner showing void. This is the position:

North
♠ A
♡ 5
♢ —
♣ 8 7 6

West
♠ J
♡ K Q 10 8
♢ —
♣ —

East
♠ —
♡ 7 6 3
♢ 10
♣ J

South
♠ 10
♡ A J 3 2
♢ —
♣ —

Declarer ruffs another club with the ten of spades. If I were to overruff the club and lead the king of hearts, declarer would win the ace of hearts, ruff a heart in dummy, and win the last two clubs. Not me. Once again, I decline to overruff.

Declarer plays the ace of hearts, ruffs a heart in dummy with the ace of spades, and continues with a high club. This time, I ruff. The king of hearts is the setting trick, so Four Spades is down one, Doubled.

The complete hand:

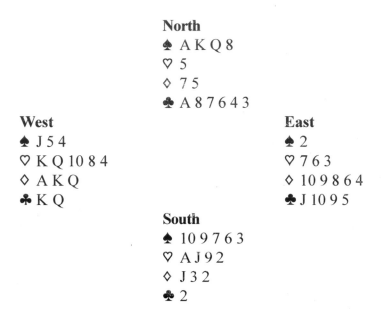

North
♠ A K Q 8
♡ 5
◇ 7 5
♣ A 8 7 6 4 3

West
♠ J 5 4
♡ K Q 10 8 4
◇ A K Q
♣ K Q

East
♠ 2
♡ 7 6 3
◇ 10 9 8 6 4
♣ J 10 9 5

South
♠ 10 9 7 6 3
♡ A J 9 2
◇ J 3 2
♣ 2

After the hand was over, partner asks, "How come you didn't overruff the third round of clubs? We could have set them two tricks, Doubled."

Hand 29

A VIEW OF SELF EMPLOYMENT

There are several advantages to being self employed. As an attorney, I can work mornings, afternoons, or evenings. And if I want, I can take the afternoon off once in a while (5 days a week) and play bridge.

Playing rubber bridge, I hold the following hand as South.

♠ A 9 3   ♡ K 8   ◊ K Q 9 7   ♣ A 9 6 5

I open the bidding with One No-Trump. West Passes and partner, sitting North, raises me to Three No-Trump, which all Pass.

The bidding has been:

NORTH	EAST	SOUTH	WEST
—	—	1NT	Pass
3NT	Pass	Pass	Pass

West leads the jack of hearts and North puts down this dummy:

North
♠ K 7 4
♡ A 5
◊ A 10 8 6
♣ 10 8 7 3

South
♠ A 9 3
♡ K 8
◊ K Q 9 7
♣ A 9 6 5

Three No-Trump is an excellent contract. I should be able to win nine tricks, consisting of two spades, two hearts, four diamonds and a club. Three No-Trump can be set only if one of my opponents holds four diamonds to the jack. Even then, I can make Three No-Trump if I can guess which opponent holds the long diamonds.

I see two possible lines of play. I can play the ace and another club. Then, if the clubs divide four-one, I could play the hand with the singleton club to be long in diamonds.

Alternatively, I can play the ace, king and another spade. Then, if the spades divide five-two, I could play the hand with the doubleton spade to hold the long diamonds.

Most likely, however, the clubs will divide three-two and the spades four-three. With normal breaks in clubs and spades, neither line of play will provide me with much information regarding the distribution of the East and West hands.

Playing the spades, however, appears to be the better line, for after playing three rounds of spades, I should gain some insights regarding my opponent's hands even if the spades divide four-three.

I win the king of hearts in hand and play the ace, king and another spade. West shows with the Q-10-8 of spades, winning the third round. East shows with the 6-5-2 of spades.

West continues with the ten of hearts to dummy's ace, East playing low. It's time now to consider the distribution of the hands. From the play so far, it appears that West began with either four or five hearts. If West held six hearts, then East would have dropped the queen of hearts under dummy's ace, to avoid blocking the suit.

If West holds the missing jack of spades, then his original holding in spades would have been the Q-J-10-8. With such strong spades, West probably would have led a spade, even if he held five hearts J-10-9-x-x. It's likely, therefore, that West began with three spades, not four.

If West holds a singleton diamond, then his distribution would be 3-5-1-4 and East would be 4-4-4-1. On the other hand, if West holds four diamonds, then his distribution would be 3-4-4-2 and East would be 4-5-1-3.

It's far more likely that West's distribution is 3-4-4-2 rather than 3-5-1-4. Likewise, it's more likely that East's distribution is 4-5-1-3 rather than 4-4-4-1. If either of my opponents holds four diamonds, it will be West, not East. I therefore play the king and queen of diamonds from hand.

Sure enough, West holds four diamonds to the jack and East has a singleton. I lead a third round of diamonds, finessing the ten, so I make Three No-Trump.

The complete hand:

North
♠ K 7 4
♡ A 5
♢ A 10 8 6
♣ 10 8 7 3

West
♠ Q 10 8
♡ J 10 9 4
♢ J 5 4 2
♣ J 2

East
♠ J 6 5 2
♡ Q 7 6 3 2
♢ 3
♣ K Q 4

South
♠ A 9 3
♡ K 8
♢ K Q 9 7
♣ A 9 6 5

I have a winning day at bridge and I return to my condo feeling quite good about my career as an attorney and the additional income I receive from playing rubber bridge. I then learn that there are some negative aspects to being self employed. I receive a letter from the Internal Revenue Service informing me that it has decided to audit my most recent income tax return.

Hand 30

MY FAVORITE HISTORICAL FIGURE

Students of American history frequently have a favorite historical figure. For some it is Patrick Henry. Others select George Washington, Thomas Jefferson or Abraham Lincoln. And me? I'll tell you later, dear reader, who my favorite historical figure is.

Playing rubber bridge, I hold the following hand as South:

♠ A K 4   ♡ 2   ♢ A K 9 8 6 5 3   ♣ 9 5

Partner, sitting North, opens the bidding with One Heart. East bids Two Spades, weak, and I bid Three Diamonds. West Passes and partner bids Three Hearts. East Passes and it is my bid.

If partner has a fit in diamonds, it's likely that we can make Six Diamonds. On the other hand, if partner has a singleton diamond, then Three No-Trump may be the best contract.

I bid Three No-Trump, hoping that partner will bid again. Partner, however, Passes so Three No-Trump becomes the final contract.

The Bidding:

NORTH	EAST	SOUTH	WEST
1 ♡	2 ♠	3 ◊	Pass
3 ♡	Pass	3NT	Pass
Pass	Pass		

West leads the nine of spades and North puts down this dummy:

North
♠ 5 3
♡ K Q 10 9 7 3
◊ Q
♣ A 10 8 4

South
♠ A K 4
♡ 2
◊ A K 9 8 6 5 3
♣ 9 5

East plays the ten of spades and I win the king. It looks normal now to lead a diamond to dummy's queen and then continue with the king and queen of hearts. With this line of play, I can make Three No-Trump if the diamonds break three-two or the jack of hearts is doubleton in either hand.

If the diamonds break three-two, I will win two spades, a heart, seven diamonds and a club, for a total of eleven tricks. But if the diamonds break four-one and the jack of hearts fails to fall doubleton, Three No-Trump will be set.

I see another line of play. Instead of playing a diamond to dummy's queen, I could play the ace and king of diamonds and continue with the nine of diamonds. This line of play would allow me to make Three No-Trump when the diamonds break three-two and also allow me to make Three No-Trump when the diamonds break four-one with either the jack or ten singleton. And if the diamonds fail to break, I can still make Three No-Trump if the hearts lie favorably, by finessing dummy's ten of hearts.

At rubber bridge, the focus is upon making your contract, not on making overtricks. I therefore play the ace and king of diamonds. Bad news. East shows with a singleton diamond, West having started with four diamonds jack-ten.

I have one last chance. I lead a heart to dummy's ten. Good news this time, for East wins the ace of hearts. The hearts break three-three, so I make Four No-Trump.

The complete hand:

North
♠ 5 3
♡ K Q 10 9 7 3
◊ Q
♣ A 10 8 4

West
♠ 9 6
♡ J 8 4
◊ J 10 7 4
♣ K 6 3 2

East
♠ Q J 10 8 7 2
♡ A 6 5
◊ 2
♣ Q J 7

South
♠ A K 4
♡ 2
◊ A K 9 8 6 5 3
♣ 9 5

I have a good day at rubber bridge and win three hundred dollars. After the session is over I place three miniature portraits of my favorite historical figure, Benjamin Franklin, into my wallet.

Hand 31

MY LUCKY DAY

Playing rubber bridge, I hold the following hand as South:

♠ Q J 2   ♡ K 5 2   ◇ A K   ♣ A Q 8 7 4

Partner, sitting North, opens the bidding with One Spade. This is my lucky day. I wish we were playing for higher stakes. East Passes and I respond Two Clubs. West Passes and partner rebids Two Hearts. I bid Three Spades and partner, running on empty, bids Four Spades. No matter, I'm pressing on to slam.

I bid Four No-Trump, Blackwood. Partner responds Five Diamonds, one ace only. It appears that we belong in either Six Spades or Six No-Trump. Before placing the contract, I stop to consider several hands which North may hold given his bidding. North ought to hold one of the following hands:

1. ♠ K x x x x   ♡ A Q x x x   ◇ x   ♣ K x

2. ♠ A K x x x   ♡ Q J x x   ◇ x x   ♣ K x

3. ♠ A K x x x   ♡ Q J x x   ◇ Q x x ♣ x

4. ♠ K x x x x   ♡ A Q x x   ◇ Q J x ♣ x

5. ♠ K x x x x   ♡ A Q x x   ◇ x x   ♣ K x

With any of these hands, Six No-Trump is a better contract than Six Spades, for there are no extra tricks to be made with spades as trump. And if the spades break poorly, I may still be able to make Six No-Trump by bringing home the clubs and hearts. I therefore bid Six No-Trump, which all Pass.

The bidding has been:

NORTH	EAST	SOUTH	WEST
1 ♠	Pass	2 ♣	Pass
2 ♡	Pass	3 ♠	Pass
4 ♠	Pass	4NT	Pass
5 ◊	Pass	6NT	Pass
Pass	Pass		

West leads the jack of diamonds and North puts down this dummy:

North
♠ K 8 7 6 4
♡ A Q 8 4
◊ 6 3
♣ K 3

South
♠ Q J 2
♡ K 5 2
◊ A K
♣ A Q 8 7 4

Six No-Trump is definitely a better contract than Six Spades. If the spades break three-two, I have twelve top tricks. And if the spades break four-one, I still may be able to win twelve tricks.

There's some advantage to be had by leading toward the queen-jack of spades, so I win the king of diamonds, enter dummy with the queen of hearts, and lead a low spade from dummy. East plays low and I play the queen, which holds.

I continue with a club to dummy's king and another spade from dummy. East plays low again, I play the jack and West shows void, discarding a small diamond. That's annoying.

I can still make Six No-Trump if the clubs break, so I play the ace and queen of clubs, pitching a spade from dummy. East follows to the ace of clubs, but on the queen of clubs he shows out, pitching a diamond.

I continue with a fourth round of clubs to West's jack, pitching another spade from dummy. East also pitches a spade. West wins the jack of clubs and continues with another diamond to East's queen and my king.

This is the position:

North
♠ K
♡ A 8 4
◊ —
♣ —

West
♠ —
♡ 7
◊ 10 9 7
♣ —

East
♠ A
♡ J 10 9
◊ —
♣ —

South
♠ 2
♡ K 5
◊ —
♣ 8

I lead my last club, pitching dummy's king of spades, and East is squeezed. If East pitches the ace of spades, my deuce of spades will be high. And if he pitches a heart, I will play the king and ace of hearts and dummy's last heart will be good.

The complete hand:

> **North**
> ♠ K 8 7 6 4
> ♡ A Q 8 4
> ◊ 6 3
> ♣ K 3

West
♠ 3
♡ 7 6
◊ J 10 9 7 5 4
♣ J 10 9 5

East
♠ A 10 9 5
♡ J 10 9 3
◊ Q 8 2
♣ 6 2

> **South**
> ♠ Q J 2
> ♡ K 5 2
> ◊ A K
> ♣ A Q 8 7 4

Six No-Trump cannot be set. If East wins the ace of spades, declarer has twelve tricks consisting of four spades, three hearts, two diamonds and three clubs.

Hand 32

THE MAN FROM NEW YORK

My partner this rubber is a man from New York visiting Los Angeles on a business trip. I've never played bridge with him before and his methods are unknown to me.

Sitting West, I hold:

♠ Q 7 5   ♡ Q J 10 8 2   ◇ 6 5 3   ♣ 7 3

North, on my left, opens the bidding with One Diamond and partner Passes. Things are looking really grim. Sure enough, North-South bid Six Spades on this auction.

The Bidding:

NORTH	EAST	SOUTH	WEST
1 ◇	Pass	1 ♠	Pass
2 ♠	Pass	4NT	Pass
5 ♠	Pass	6 ♠	Pass
Pass	Pass		

I lead the queen of hearts and North puts down this dummy:

                    North
                    ♠ 9 6 3 2
                    ♡ A 5
                    ◇ A 10 9 4
                    ♣ A J 8
    West
    ♠ Q 7 5
    ♡ Q J 10 8 2
    ◇ 6 5 3
    ♣ 7 3

Declarer wins the ace of hearts in dummy, ruffs a heart and then plays the ace and king of spades. Partner follows to the first spade but on the second spade partner shows void, pitching a heart.

Declarer next plays the ace, king, and queen of clubs. There's no need for me to ruff the queen of clubs, so I discard a heart. Declarer continues with a spade which I win with the queen. Partner discards another heart.

It looks right now to lead a diamond, for a heart would allow declarer to ruff in dummy and sluff a diamond from hand. But before leading a diamond, I stop to count declarer's hand.

South was dealt five spades and one heart. Partner played the 2, 4, and 6 of clubs under the ace, king, and queen, which shows that partner began with an odd number of clubs, undoubtedly five. Partner's distribution must be 1-5-2-5 and South's distribution must be 5-1-4-3.

Most likely, declarer holds four diamonds K-J-x-x opposite dummy's A-10-9-6. A diamond lead now will locate partner's queen of diamonds and allow declarer to make Six Spades. But a heart lead, giving declarer a sluff and a ruff, won't help declarer at all. Declarer will still have to guess the diamonds correctly in order to make Six Spades. I therefore lead a heart, expecting the complete hand to be:

North
♠ 9 6 3 2
♡ A 5
♢ A 10 9 4
♣ A J 8

West
♠ Q 7 5
♡ Q J 10 8 2
♢ 6 5 3
♣ 7 3

East
♠ 4
♡ K 9 6 4 3
♢ Q 7
♣ 10 9 6 4 2

South
♠ A K J 10 8
♡ 7
♢ K J 8 2
♣ K Q 5

Unfortunately, the hand was not as I expected. Declarer's distribution was 5-1-3-4, not 5-1-4-3. My heart lead allows declarer to make Six Spades by ruffing in dummy and sluffing a diamond from hand.

The complete hand:

North
♠ 9 6 3 2
♡ A 5
◊ A 10 9 4
♣ A J 8

West
♠ Q J 5
♡ Q J 10 8 2
◊ 6 5 3
♣ 7 3

East
♠ 4
♡ K 9 6 4 3
◊ Q J 7
♣ 9 6 4 2

South
♠ A K J 10 8
♡ 7
◊ K 8 2
♣ K Q 10 5

Declarer makes Six Spades if the queen and jack of diamonds are held separately, for after West wins the queen of trumps, West must lead a diamond. South played the hand well by not cashing the ten of clubs. As a consequence of declarer not cashing the ten of clubs, I was unable to count South's distribution correctly.

Partner, of course, should have played high-low on the clubs, showing four. If partner had counted the clubs for me, I would have been able to count declarer's hand correctly. After winning the queen of spades I would then have returned a diamond rather than a heart.

North-South take great pleasure in making Six Spades. Partner, on the other hand, is quite upset and shrieks, "How could you give declarer a sluff and a ruff. You're the worst player I've ever had the misfortune to play bridge with." So saying, the man from New York paid his losses and quit the game.

Hand 33

THE GORILLA

My right hand opponent has gigantic muscles. His arms are thicker than my legs. Players at the bridge club affectionately call him the Gorilla. He's so huge, he'd make a great football player. Maybe he takes steroids. Oh well, it's none of my business.

Playing rubber bridge, I hold the following hand as South, againt the Gorilla:

♠ Q J 10 7 4 3   ♡ K 8   ◇ K 7   ♣ A Q 6

I open the bidding with One Spade. West Passes and partner considers his hand for several seconds. Partner then bids Six Spades, which all Pass.

The Bidding:

NORTH	EAST	SOUTH	WEST
—	—	1 ♠	Pass
6 ♠	Pass	Pass	Pass

West leads the jack of hearts. North, full of pride, puts down this dummy for me:

North
♠ A K 9 8 5
♡ A 3
◇ A J 3
♣ 7 4 2

South
♠ Q J 10 7 4 3
♡ K 8
◇ K 7
♣ A Q 6

I have six spade tricks, two hearts, two diamonds and a club, for a total of eleven top tricks. At first glance, it appears that Six Spades depends upon a successful finesse in either diamonds or clubs. But I adopt a line of play which slightly improves the odds.

I win the ace of hearts in dummy and cash the ace of spades. Both opponents follow to the spade. I continue with a heart to my king and then play the king of diamonds and a second diamond toward dummy's ace-jack, West playing low.

I don't need to take the diamond finesse. If West holds the queen of diamonds, I can always make Six Spades. I win the ace of diamonds in dummy and continue with the jack of diamonds, planning to pitch a club from hand if East fails to play the queen. If West wins the jack of diamonds with the queen, he will be endplayed and forced to lead a club into my ace-queen.

Unfortunately, East covers dummy's jack of diamonds with the queen. I ruff, lead a spade to dummy, and continue with a low club toward my ace-queen.

If I catch East napping with a low club, I will duck the club to West. Unfortunately, East plays the nine of clubs. There's no use in taking the club finesse now. I win the ace of clubs, enter dummy with a spade, and lead another club toward my queen. East plays the ten of clubs, I play the queen, and West wins the king. Fortunately, West began with a doubleton king of clubs. West is forced to play either a heart or a diamond, giving me a ruff and a sluff, so I make Six Spades.

The complete hand:

North
♠ A K 9 8 5
♡ A 3
◊ A J 3
♣ 7 4 2

West
♠ 6
♡ J 10 9 7 4
◊ 9 8 6 4 2
♣ K 8

East
♠ 2
♡ Q 6 5 2
◊ Q 10 5
♣ J 10 9 5 3

South
♠ Q J 10 7 4 3
♡ K 8
◊ K 7
♣ A Q 6

The normal line of play is to take the diamond finesse and then take the club finesse. If either finesse wins, declarer makes Six Spades.

But the recommended line of play gains whenever East holds the queen of diamonds doubleton or West holds the king of clubs doubleton. At rubber bridge, every additional chance to make your contract helps.

After several hours of rubber bridge, I am the only winner. Two of the other players lose a hundred dollars each and pay their losses. The Gorilla loses five dollars.

"Give me a chance to get even," says the Gorilla. "Arm wrestle me, double or nothing. To make it fair, I'll let you use both arms."

This seems fair enough to me and I accept the Gorilla's challenge. I sit down opposite the Gorilla and lock arms. We begin to wrestle, my two arms against his one. I lean into it with all my strength. The Gorilla, however, doesn't budge an inch.

"You can start any time," he says. "I did start, a minute ago," I protest, somewhat hopelessly. And then, ever so easily, the Gorilla, using only one arm, forces both of my arms to the table.

Hand 34

THE MARRYING MAN

After three failed marriages, I came to the conclusion that my wives were not at fault. No doubt my marriages failed because I stayed out all night, playing bridge, instead of coming home. What I need is a wife who thrives on neglect.

Playing rubber bridge, I hold the following hand as South:

♠ A K 7   ♡ K Q 2   ◊ 8 7 4   ♣ A 8 7 5

Partner and I bid Three No-Trump on the following auction:

NORTH	EAST	SOUTH	WEST
—	—	—	Pass
Pass	Pass	1NT	Pass
3NT	Pass	Pass	Pass

West leads the jack of spades and partner puts down this dummy:

North
♠ Q 6 5
♡ J 10 8
◊ Q J 10 9 3
♣ K 9

South
♠ A K 7
♡ K Q 2
◊ 8 7 4
♣ A 8 7 5

Three No-Trump is a good contract. I should be able to win three spades, two hearts, three diamonds and two clubs, for a total of ten tricks. But West may hold five spades. If so, my opponents may be able to establish the spades and win two spades, a heart and two diamonds, for a total of five tricks, before I am able to set up both the diamonds and the hearts.

Since West is a passed hand, he can't hold the jack of spades, the ace of hearts and the ace-king of diamonds. The most West can hold is the jack of spades and two of the three missing honors.

It seems normal to win the first spade and play the diamonds rather than the hearts. But I see a problem with attacking the diamonds first. If East wins the first diamond, the defense will be able to set Three No-Trump if West holds five spades, a diamond honor and the ace of hearts.

But if I play the hearts first, the defense will be able to defeat Three No-Trump only if East holds the ace of hearts and West holds both the ace and king of diamonds. It's more likely that West holds the ace of hearts and a diamond honor rather than both the ace and king of diamonds.

I therefore lead a low heart rather than a diamond. Dummy's jack wins. I then play the diamonds and make Three No-Trump.

The complete hand:

North
♠ Q 6 5
♡ J 10 8
◊ Q J 10 9 3
♣ K 9

West
♠ J 10 9 8 2
♡ A 5 4
◊ K 6 2
♣ J 4

East
♠ 4 3
♡ 9 7 4 3
◊ A 5
♣ Q 10 6 3 2

South
♠ A K 7
♡ K Q 2
◊ 8 7 4
♣ A 8 7 5

After the hand is over, my girl friend telephones me. "Come over soon," she says. "There's a new episode of The Practice on television tonight at 10:00 p.m."

"Why don't you record it on the VCR," I reply, "Then we can watch it at midnight, after I'm through playing bridge."

Hand 35

THE GIRL FRIEND

As a attorney, I put in 30 hours of work per week. I spend another 40 hours a week playing bridge. This doesn't leave me much time to spend with my girl friend.

Playing rubber bridge, I hold the following hand as East:

♠ 4 2   ♡ 9 8 3   ◊ Q 10 9 3   ♣ K Q J 8

North-South bid Four Hearts on this auction:

The Bidding:

NORTH	EAST	SOUTH	WEST
—	—	1 ♠	Pass
1NT	Pass	2 ♡	Pass
3 ♡	Pass	4 ♡	Pass
Pass	Pass		

Partner leads the jack of hearts and North puts down this dummy:

North
♠ 5
♡ 7 6 5 2
◊ A J 7 2
♣ A 7 6 3

East
♠ 4 2
♡ 9 8 3
◊ Q 10 9 3
♣ K Q J 8

Partner is undoubtedly well fixed in spades. He's led a trump to cut down on the spade ruffs in dummy.

Declarer wins the jack of hearts in hand with the queen. He then cashes the ace of spades, ruffs a spade in dummy, returns to hand with the king of hearts and ruffs another second spade in dummy. On the spades, partner plays the nine, ten and queen.

The obvious play is to overruff dummy's seven of hearts and return the king of clubs. But before overruffing the spade, I stop to count declarer's hand.

Partner's play of the spades shows that he began with the K-Q-10-9 of spades. This gives declarer six spades ace-jack. Declarer's hearts are the A-K-Q-x. South should hold one of the following hands:

1. ♠ A J x x x x ♡ A K Q x ◇ x ♣ x x

2. ♠ A J x x x x ♡ A K Q x ◇ x x ♣ x

If I overruff the spade, declarer will be left with the two remaining trumps. Declarer will then be able to return to hand by ruffing a club or a diamond and concede a spade to partner's king. Declarer will later ruff a club or diamond to hand and win the last two spades, for a total of ten tricks.

But if I discard a club or a diamond on the spade instead of over-ruffing, declarer won't be able to win the last two spades, for I will still have a trump to ruff when declarer plays high spades from hand. Declarer will be able to win only three spades, four hearts, a diamond and a clubs, for nine tricks. I therefore discard a diamond rather than overruff the spade.

Declarer continues with the ace of clubs, a club ruff to hand, and concedes a spade to partner's king. Partner continues with another club, which declarer ruffs with his last trump. Declarer plays a high spade, which I ruff. The defense later wins a club and a diamond, so Four Hearts is down one.

The complete hand:

North
- ♠ 5
- ♡ 7 6 5 2
- ◇ A J 7 2
- ♣ A 7 6 3

West
- ♠ K Q 10 9
- ♡ J 10
- ◇ K 8 6
- ♣ 10 9 5 2

East
- ♠ 4 2
- ♡ 9 8 3
- ◇ Q 10 9 3
- ♣ K Q J 8

South
- ♠ A J 8 7 6 3
- ♡ A K Q 4
- ◇ 5 4
- ♣ 4

Four Hearts can be made. Declarer should win the first heart and duck a spade. Declarer wins the second heart in hand, ruffs a spade in dummy, returns to hand with the ace of hearts and plays the ace and another spade. This leaves South with the last trump and two high spades, and declarer wins a total of ten tricks.

After the hand is over, my girl friend telephones and asks me to take her out to a movie. I resist, telling her that I took her out to a movie last week.

"Please," she says.

"Oh, all right," I say. That's what happens when you have a girl friend. You have to sacrifice an evening of bridge once in a while to make her happy.

Hand 36

SEARCH FOR AN INTRUDER

This hand comes from my college years, when I was short of money and sincerely appreciated professional bridge dates. My patron is a middle aged woman. I pick her up at her home and drive her to a Regional Bridge Tournament.

Partner and I bid Six Hearts on this hand:

The Bidding:

NORTH	EAST	SOUTH	WEST
—	—	1 ♡	Pass
3NT**	Pass	6 ♡	Pass
Pass	Pass		

**raise to 4H, no singleton

North
- ♠ 6 3
- ♡ K 9 8
- ◊ Q J 7 3
- ♣ A Q 7 3

South
- ♠ A
- ♡ A Q J 10 7
- ◊ K 4 2
- ♣ K 5 4 2

West leads the four of hearts. The trump lead does me no harm. There's some advantage to be gained by leading the diamonds from the king toward the queen-jack, for West may hold a doubleton ace, so I win three rounds of hearts, ending in hand. West pitches a spade on the third heart.

I lead a diamond from hand to dummy's jack, which holds, then return to hand with the ace of spades and lead another diamond. West thinks for a while, then ducks, and dummy's queen wins.

I can make Six Hearts if the diamonds are three-three or if the clubs break three-two. But it's likely that the diamonds are four-two. And it's possible that the clubs will break four-one rather than three-two.

If I play a diamond, then West will win the ace of diamonds and return another diamond. That would destroy any chance for a club-diamond squeeze. How should I proceed?

I have it! I play dummy's spade and pitch my king of diamonds. This permits me to later enter dummy with a club and ruff a diamond. I will then make Six Hearts if the diamonds break three-three, the clubs break three-two, or with a squeeze if West holds four clubs and four diamonds.

West wins the king of spades and returns the ace of diamonds, East showing void. This is the position after I ruff the diamond and play my last trump.

North
♠ —
♡ —
◊ 7
♣ A Q 7 3

West
♠ —
♡ —
◊ 10
♣ J 9 8 6

East
♠ Q J 9 7
♡ —
◊ —
♣ 10

South
♠ —
♡ 10
◊ —
♣ K 5 4 2

West is squeezed in the minors, so I make Six Hearts.

The complete hand:

North
♠ 6 3
♡ K 9 8
◇ Q J 7 3
♣ A Q 7 3

West
♠ K 10 8
♡ 4 2
◇ A 10 9 6
♣ J 9 8 6

East
♠ Q J 9 7 5 4 2
♡ 6 5 3
◇ 8 5
♣ 10

South
♠ A
♡ A Q J 10 7
◇ K 4 2
♣ K 5 4 2

After two sessions of bridge, I drive my partner to her home. She asks me to come inside, "to look for intruders". I enter her home and look in every room. In spite of my best efforts, I am unable to locate any intruders.

During the course of my inspection I notice a twenty dollar bill lying on her dining room table. "What's the twenty dollar bill for?" I ask.

"I leave the twenty dollar bill out on purpose," she replies. "Then if I come home at night and the twenty dollar bill is still there, I feel certain that no one has broken into my home."

"That's a very good idea," I say, complimenting my patron on her strategy.

I wait until she's not looking, then grab the twenty dollar bill. No, dear reader, I'm not a thief. I leave two ten dollar bills in place of the twenty.

Hand 37

THE MAGICIAN

Sometimes when I play bridge, I'm a magician. I create an illusion that befuddles my opponents. Consider this hand, dear reader.

Playing duplicate bridge, partner and I reach Six Spades on the following auction:

The Bidding:

NORTH	EAST	SOUTH	WEST
—	—	1 ♠	Pass
6 ♠	Pass	Pass	Pass

North
- ♠ Q J 10 7 2
- ♡ 10 9 3
- ◇ A K 7
- ♣ A K

South
- ♠ A K 9 8 4 3
- ♡ K
- ◇ 8 3
- ♣ Q 5 4 2

West leads the queen of diamonds.

I have twelve top tricks. My only chance for an overtrick is to win a trick with the king of hearts. The normal play is to pull trumps and lead a heart toward the king. If East holds the ace and ducks, I can make thirteen tricks. But if West holds the ace of hearts, he will win the ace and hold me to twelve tricks.

But I see a way to create an illusion. I win the queen of diamonds in dummy and lead a spade to my king. Both opponents follow to the spade.

I continue with the king of diamonds and a diamond ruff, followed by the ace and king of clubs. I drop the queen of clubs under the king, making it appear that I hold a doubleton club.

This is the position when I lead a low heart from dummy:

```
                         North
                         ♠ Q J 10 7
                         ♥ 10 9 3
                         ◊ —
                         ♣ —

West                                        East
♠ —                                         ♠ —
♥ A J 4                                      ♥ Q 8 7 6 5 2
◊ J 10                                       ◊ —
♣ J 8                                        ♣ 9

                         South
                         ♠ A 9 8 4 3
                         ♥ K
                         ◊ —
                         ♣ 5 4
```

West considers winning the king of hearts with the ace, but he believes that my distribution is 6-3-2-2 and that I hold K-Q-x in hearts. He ducks the king of hearts, so I make an overtrick.

The complete hand:

```
                         North
                         ♠ Q J 10 7 2
                         ♥ 10 9 3
                         ◊ A K 7
                         ♣ A K

West                                        East
♠ 6                                         ♠ 5
♥ A J 4                                      ♥ Q 8 7 6 5 2
◊ Q J 10 4 2                                 ◊ 9 6 5
♣ J 8 7 6                                    ♣ 10 9 3

                         South
                         ♠ A K 9 8 4 3
                         ♥ K
                         ◊ 8 3
                         ♣ Q 5 4 2
```

West should have seen through the illusion which I created by playing the queen of clubs under the king. If East's clubs were 10-9-5-4-3, East would play the 3 and 4 of clubs under dummy's ace and king. On the actual hand, East's clubs are the 10-9-3 and he plays the 3 and 9 of clubs under dummy's ace and king. If West is watching the club spots, he should conclude that East does not hold five clubs.

Hand 38

CALIFORNIA RULES

Whenever I play duplicate bridge with my girlfriend, we agree to play California Rules i.e., if we win, then we engage in undercover activities after the game.

My girlfriend and I bid to Six Hearts on the following auction:

NORTH	EAST	SOUTH	WEST
1 ◊	Pass	1 ♡	Pass
3 ♡	Pass	4 ♣	Pass
4 ◊	Pass	6 ♡	Pass
Pass	Pass		

West leads the jack of spades and partner puts down this dummy:

North
♠ A
♡ Q J 9 6
◊ A K 8 7 6 4
♣ 6 3

South
♠ K 7 5
♡ K 10 8 7 5
◊ 5 3
♣ A K 8

Six Hearts is an excellent contract. I see two lines of play. The first line of play is to pull trumps and attempt to set up dummy's diamonds. With this line of play, I can make Six Hearts if the trumps split two-two or if the diamonds divide three-two. But Six Hearts will be set if the hearts break three-one and the diamonds break four-one.

The second line of play is to simply ruff a spade and a club in dummy. This line of play appears better, so I shall give up on dummy's diamonds.

I win the ace of spades in dummy. I could lead a trump at this point, but I don't want my opponents to be able to play the ace and another heart before I ruff both a spade and a club in dummy.

I lead a club to hand at trick two, cash the king of spades, pitching a diamond from dummy, and ruff a spade. I continue with another club to hand and ruff a club in dummy. I then lead the queen of hearts from dummy, which holds, leaving this position:

North
♠ —
♡ J
♦ A K 8 7 6
♣ —

South
♠ —
♡ K 10 8 7
♦ 5 3
♣ —

Most likely, one of my opponents holds three hearts to the ace. It looks normal now to lead another heart and force out the ace. After pulling the remaining small trump, I can claim Six Hearts.

But I foresee a problem with playing another heart now. The diamonds may break four-one. If so, the opponent with three trumps, most likely East, will win the ace of hearts and return a diamond, pinning me in dummy. With dummy holding nothing but diamonds, I would be forced to play a second diamond from dummy, which East would ruff.

To avert a possible diamond ruff, I cash the ace of diamonds before playing dummy's jack of hearts. This strips East of his singleton diamond. East wins the ace of hearts, but he's unable now to pin me in dummy. East returns a spade, which I ruff. I then play the king of hearts, extracting East's last trump, and claim twelve tricks.

My precautions were necessary, for this was the complete hand:

North
♠ A
♡ Q J 9 6
◇ A K 8 7 6 4
♣ 6 3

West
♠ J 10 9 6 4
♡ 3
◇ Q J 9 2
♣ Q 10 4

East
♠ Q 8 3 2
♡ A 4 2
◇ 10
♣ J 9 7 5 2

South
♠ K 7 5
♡ K 10 8 7 5
◇ 5 3
♣ A K 8

Some bridge players have dubbed the play of the ace of diamonds a "Dentist's Coup." Dentist's coups, which extract a dangerous exit card from an opponent's hand, come up from time to time, but they are often overlooked.

Another dentist's coup, one that I overlooked, occurred on the following hand:

North
♠ 8 7
♡ 5
◇ A K 10 6 4
♣ A K 9 7 3

West
♠ K 3 2
♡ K Q 9 3
◇ 8
♣ Q 10 8 6 5

East
♠ 6
♡ J 10 8 7 6 4
◇ Q J 5 3 2
♣ J

South
♠ A Q J 10 9 5 4
♡ A 2
◇ 9 7
♣ 4 2

Playing in Six Spades, I won the ace of hearts, ruffed a heart, and led the ace and queen of spades. West won the king of spades and returned the queen of clubs to dummy's ace. Believing that West might hold a singleton club, I attempted to exit dummy by playing the ace and king of diamonds. West ruffed the second diamond, so I went down one in Six Spades.

The correct play is to ruff a heart in dummy, play the ace of clubs and ace of diamonds, and then the ace and queen of spades. West wins the king of spades, but no matter how West continues declarer can return to hand, pull West's last trump and claim twelve tricks, making Six Spades.

***

We place second overall, which isn't good enough to qualify for undercover activities under California Rules. But my girlfriend is in a good mood, so I get lucky anyway.

Hand 39

THE CHESS PLAYER

My partner this rubber is a grand master at chess. But at the bridge table, he has a room temperature I.Q. My opponents, on the other hand, are quite competent.

Sitting West, I hold:

♠ J 8   ♡ J 9 2   ◊ K J 6 3   ♣ Q 9 4 3

South, on my right, opens the bidding with One Spade. I Pass and North makes a limit raise of Three Spades. Partner Passes and South bids Four Spades, which all Pass.

The Bidding:

NORTH	EAST	SOUTH	WEST
—	—	1 ♠	Pass
3 ♠	Pass	4 ♠	Pass
Pass			

I lead a low club and North puts down this dummy:

                          North
                          ♠ K 9 7 5
                          ♡ A Q 4
                          ◊ 7 5 4 2
                          ♣ J 6
        West
        ♠ J 8
        ♡ J 9 2
        ◊ K J 6 3
        ♣ Q 9 4 3

North plays the jack of clubs from dummy, partner covers with the king, and South plays the five. Partner returns the seven of clubs and declarer wins the ace. The deuce of clubs is missing and it's likely that partner began with five clubs.

Declarer plays the ace of spades and a spade to dummy's king. Partner shows void on the second spade, pitching the deuce of clubs. Declarer plays a diamond to his ace, partner playing the nine. Declarer continues with the eight of diamonds from hand and it is my play.

Declarer's play of the diamonds makes it clear that partner holds the queen of diamonds. Partner must also hold the king of hearts, for if declarer held the king of hearts, he would have eleven top tricks.

If partner holds the queen third of diamonds, then declarer's distribution will be 6-3-2-2. In that case, I should let partner win the second round of diamonds and return a third diamond, which declarer will ruff. Declarer would then be forced to play the hearts himself, and the defense should win two heart tricks.

But it's likely that partner holds the queen of diamonds doubleton. If so, declarer's distribution will be 6-2-3-2. If I were to play low on the diamond, then partner would win the queen of diamonds and be endplayed, forced to lead a heart into dummy's ace-queen, or a club, which would give declarer a sluff and a ruff. I play the king of diamonds, which prevents East from being endplayed. Sure enough, partner drops the queen of diamonds under my king.

I must shift to a heart now, for cashing the jack of diamonds would set up dummy's seven of diamonds for a heart pitch. Ordinarily, it would be correct to lead a low heart. But if I were to lead a low heart, declarer could duck in dummy and partner would be endplayed after winning the heart.

Instead of leading a low heart, I lead the jack of hearts. If declarer holds the ten of hearts, he will make Four Spades. But if partner holds both the king and ten of hearts, we will set Four Spades. Declarer plays the queen of hearts from dummy and partner wins the king. Partner returns a low heart to my nine, which forces dummy's ace. Declarer later concedes a trick to my jack of diamonds, so Four Spades is down one.

The complete hand:

North
♠ K 9 7 5
♡ A Q 4
◇ 7 5 4 2
♣ J 6

West
♠ J 8
♡ J 9 2
◇ K J 6 3
♣ Q 9 4 3

East
♠ 3
♡ K 10 8 6 5
◇ Q 9
♣ K 10 8 7 2

South
♠ A Q 10 6 4 2
♡ 7 3
◇ A 10 8
♣ A 5

Declarer played the hand well by allowing East to win the first round of clubs. By denying West an entry in clubs, declarer gained additional chances to make Four Spades. If East had held the K-Q, K-J or Q-J of diamonds doubleton, Four Spades could not be set after declarer plays the ace and another diamond.

East made two errors in the defense. The first error occurred when declarer led a low diamond from dummy. East should play the queen of diamonds rather than the nine. If declarer's diamonds had been A-J-x, declarer could play the ace and a low diamond, making Four Spades no matter how West defends.

East's second error occurred when he won the king of hearts. East should return the ten of hearts, rather than a low heart, in case declarer held the nine of hearts doubleton.

After the afternoon bridge session ends, North and I play three games of chess. I have no chance, of course, and North wins every game. When it comes to chess, I am the one with the room temperature I.Q.

Hand 40

THE COLOR OF
THE CARPET

I enter a room, stay for an hour, then leave. A friend remarks that she thought the carpet was beautiful. Well, guess what. I never saw the carpet. I couldn't tell you the color of the carpet. But when it comes to bridge, I seem to see more than most players.

Playing duplicate bridge, partner and I bid to Two Spades on the following hand:

The Bidding:

NORTH	EAST	SOUTH	WEST
—	—	—	Pass
Pass	1 ♡	1 ♠	Pass
2 ♣	Pass	Pass	Pass

North
♠ 5 3 2
♡ 7 4 3
◊ A Q 4
♣ A 8 7 6

South
♠ A K Q J 7
♡ J 10 5 2
◊ J 7 3
♣ 3

West leads the deuce of hearts. East wins the queen, king and ace of hearts, West pitching a club and a diamond. East plays a fourth round of hearts to my jack, West ruffs with the six of spades and I must decide what card to play from dummy.

Normally, it would be correct to discard a diamond. Then if the diamond finesse worked, I could ruff my third diamond in dummy, making Two Spades with an overtrick. East, however, might hold three spades and a doubleton diamond. If so, East would overruff the third round of diamonds and I would be limited to eight tricks.

West's first discard was a club, which strongly suggests that West began with five clubs. Since West has a singleton heart, West's most likely distribution is 3-1-4-5 or 2-1-5-5. If West has the king of diamonds and the club length, then I can ruff two clubs to establish a club threat against West and later squeeze West in the minors.

Playing for a squeeze against West is better than playing to ruff a diamond in dummy, for a squeeze against West will work whenever West holds the king of diamonds and five clubs, i.e., when West's distribution is either 3-1-4-5 or 2-1-5-5. Playing for a diamond ruff in dummy succeeds only when West holds the king of diamonds and West's distribution is 3-1-4-5.

In order to squeeze West in the minors, I must save three diamonds in dummy and all of dummy's clubs. So instead of discarding a club or a diamond from dummy, I underruff!

West returns a club which I win with dummy's ace. I ruff a club to hand and cash the ace and king of spades. On the second spade West shows void, pitching a diamond. I continue with a diamond to dummy's queen, which holds, and ruff another club to hand. This is the position when I cash the queen of spades:

North
♠ —
♡ —
◇ A 4
♣ 8

West
♠ —
♡ —
◇ K 10
♣ Q

East
♠ 10
♡ 9
◇ 9
♣ —

South
♠ Q
♡ —
◇ J 7
♣ —

The queen of spades squeezes West in the minors, so I make Three Spades for a very good match point score, but not a top. One ambitious East-West pair played in Three Hearts Doubled, down four.

The complete hand:

North
♠ 5 3 2
♡ 7 4 3
◇ A Q 4
♣ A 8 7 6

West
♠ 9 6
♡ 6
◇ K 10 8 6 5
♣ Q 10 5 4 2

East
♠ 10 8 4
♡ A K Q 9 8
◇ 9 2
♣ K J 9

South
♠ A K Q J 7
♡ J 10 5 2
◇ J 7 3
♣ 3

If dummy pitches a diamond on the fourth round of hearts, a diamond shift by West holds declarer to eight tricks. And if dummy pitches a club on the fourth round of hearts, West saves the diamonds, East saves the clubs and declarer is again limited to eight tricks. Only an underruff allows declarer to win nine tricks.

Hand 41

THE ODD COUPLE

When playing duplicate bridge, you sometimes encounter people that you otherwise would never meet. My left hand opponent this round is a man with several studs in his ears. He has dark green hair, cut very short. On my right is a woman with long purple hair. She is wearing a ring on each finger, and a ring in her nose. Where else could you meet a couple like these two but at a rock concert or a bridge tournament?

I say hello to each opponent, but I find the small talk somewhat awkward. It's not my practice to compliment women for their nose rings. Quite frankly, I don't know what to say.

We all take our hands out of the duplicate board and play bridge. Playing South, I hold the following hand:

♠ A 5 3 ♡ A K 10 ◇ K 10 4 ♣ A K 10 7

I open the bidding with Two No-Trump. West Passes and partner bids Six No-Trump, which all Pass.

The Bidding:

NORTH	EAST	SOUTH	WEST
—	—	2NT	Pass
6NT	Pass	Pass	Pass

West leads the queen of spades and partner puts down this dummy:

North
♠ 7 2
♡ Q 6
◇ A Q 8 7 3
♣ Q J 8 4

South
♠ A 5 3
♡ A K 10
◇ K 10 4
♣ A K 10 7

I have eleven top tricks, consisting of one spade, three hearts, three diamonds and four clubs. If the diamonds break three-two, I will be able to win all thirteen tricks.

But the diamonds may be breaking four-one. If West holds four diamonds, I can pick up the suit by running the ten of diamonds through his jack-nine fourth. If East holds the diamonds, it will be necessary to lead from a low diamond from dummy and finesse the ten.

At rubber bridge, I would duck the queen of spades. This would cost an overtrick when the diamonds split three-two, but ducking the queen of spades would make it easier for me to count the hand. At duplicate bridge, however, I can't afford to duck the queen of spades. Every North-South pair will be in Six No-Trump and it's essential to make an overtrick if possible.

I win West's queen of spades with the ace. At first sight, it appears correct to cash four rounds of clubs and then the queen, king and ace of hearts. If either opponent shows with four clubs or six hearts, I may be persuaded to play for a four-one diamond split.

Cashing the clubs first, however, is the wrong play. It's correct to play the hearts first, in order to determine whether to win the fourth round of clubs in hand or in dummy.

I play the queen, king and ace of hearts, pitching a spade from dummy. On the third round of hearts, West shows void, pitching a diamond. West began with two hearts and East began with six hearts. If anyone holds four diamonds, it will be West.

I next play the jack, queen and king of clubs, being careful to retain the ace of clubs in hand for a later entry. West shows with two clubs, discarding a spade on the third club.

West began with two hearts and two clubs. His distribution must be 5-2-4-2 or 6-2-3-2. That gives East a distribution of either 3-6-1-3 or 2-6-2-3.

West has one of these hands:

1. ♠ Q J 10 x x   ♡ x x   ◊ J 9 x x   ♣ x x

2. ♠ Q J 10 x x x   ♡ x x   ◊ J x x   ♣ x x

3. ♠ Q J 10 x x x   ♡ x x   ◊ x x x   ♣ x x

East has one of these hands:

1. ♠ K x x   ♡ J x x x x x   ◊ x   ♣ x x x

2. ♠ K x   ♡ J x x x x x   ◊ x x   ♣ x x x

3. ♠ K x   ♡ J x x x x x   ◊ J x   ♣ x x x

It's more likely that West's distribution is 5-2-4-2 rather than 6-2-3-2. And if West's distribution is 6-2-3-2, there's still a 60% chance that West will hold the jack of diamonds. In short, I believe that the best play to make Six No-Trump is to run the ten of diamonds through West rather than playing for the diamonds to split three-two. In any event, one doesn't win duplicate bridge tournaments by making ordinary plays.

I cash the king of diamonds, which gives me the slight chance of finding the jack of diamonds singleton with East, but the jack of diamonds does not fall. I then lead the ten of diamonds from hand, intending to play low if West ducks. West, however, covers the ten of diamonds with the jack. I win the queen of diamonds in dummy and East shows void. The rest is easy. I return to hand with the ace of clubs and finesse the eight of diamonds, making Six No-Trump with an overtrick, for a top score.

The complete hand:

North
♠ 7 2
♡ Q 6
◊ A Q 8 7 3
♣ Q J 8 4

West
♠ Q J 10 8 4
♡ 4 3
◊ J 9 6 2
♣ 9 3

East
♠ K 9 6
♡ J 9 8 7 5 2
◊ 5
♣ 6 5 2

South
♠ A 5 3
♡ A K 10
◊ K 10 4
♣ A K 10 7

At rubber bridge, South should duck the queen of spades lead. West will continue with the jack of spades and East will play low. Thereafter, declarer will be able to count the hands with absolute certainty, for declarer will discover that East started with the king third of spades, six hearts and three clubs.

At duplicate bridge, however, declarer must win the first spade. Most players would then continue with four rounds of clubs, but it's correct to play the hearts first. If West shows with six hearts, declarer plays three rounds of clubs, saving a high club in dummy.

If West has six hearts and three clubs, declarer should play the ace of diamonds, finesse the ten of diamonds, cash the king of diamonds and then return to dummy with the high club.

After the round is over our opponents move on to the next table. "They were a little weird," I say to my partner. "Did you notice the woman with purple hair and the nose ring? And the man had green hair."

"Jim," says my partner, "You're mistaken. The one with the green hair was a woman. They were both women."

Hand 42

A VISIT TO THE MENS ROOM

Half way through a 64 board match in a knockout teams event of a national tournament I notice a need to recycle some of the coffee I've been drinking. As soon as this hand is over, I'm going to visit the men's room. Meanwhile, partner and I bid game on the following hand:

The Bidding:

NORTH	EAST	SOUTH	WEST
Pass	Pass	2 ♣	Pass
2 ◊*	Pass	2 ♡	Pass
4 ♡**	Pass	Pass	Pass

*weak   **no ace or king

North
♠ 8 4 2
♡ 6 4 3
◊ Q J 9 7
♣ 9 7 3

South
♠ A 7
♡ A K 8 5 2
◊ A K 6
♣ A K 5

West leads the queen of spades.

If trumps break three-two, I should be able to win a spade, four hearts, four diamonds and two clubs, for a total of eleven tricks. The question is, can I make Four Hearts if the hearts break four-one?

With imp scoring, the focus in upon making your contract and overtricks are of little concern. I therefore adopt a line of play which is almost certain to make Four Hearts but disregards potential overtricks.

I win the ace of spades and duck a small heart. East wins the jack of hearts and continues with the king and another spade, which I ruff. At this point, I could play the ace and king of hearts. If the hearts break three-two, I will win a spade trick, four heart tricks, four diamond tricks and two clubs, and make Four Hearts with an overtrick. And if the hearts break four-one, I will continue with the ace, king and another diamond, making Four Hearts unless the opponent with four hearts has a doubleton diamond.

But if the defender with four hearts holds a doubleton diamond, rather than three diamonds, he will ruff the third diamond and Four Hearts will be set. To insure making ten tricks, I duck another heart. Sure enough, West wins the nine of hearts and East shows void.

Four Hearts is cold now. If West continues with another spade, I will ruff in dummy. And if West returns a diamond or a club, I will win in hand and pull West's remaining trumps, making Four Hearts.

The complete hand:

North
- ♠ 8 4 2
- ♡ 6 4 3
- ◊ Q J 9 7
- ♣ 9 7 3

West
- ♠ Q J 10 6
- ♡ Q 10 9 7
- ◊ 4 3
- ♣ Q 10 8

East
- ♠ K 9 5 3
- ♡ J
- ◊ 10 8 5 2
- ♣ J 6 4 2

South
- ♠ A 7
- ♡ A K 8 5 2
- ◊ A K 6
- ♣ A K 5

After the hand is over, I excuse myself and go to the men's room. One of the directors tags along. I enter the men's room. The director also enters the men's room and watches me as I take a leak.

"Excuse me," I say, feeling somewhat uncomfortable under the circumstances, "Are you following me?"

"Yes, I am," he replies.

"Why," I ask, hoping that the director won't tell me that he's gay and that he's developed a crush on me.

"A.C.B.L. directives require that I monitor you while you visit the men's room. This is necessary to ensure that you don't communicate any unauthorized information to your team mates about the boards you've just played," responds the director.

Hand 43

BIG BROTHER

I'm really angry. I just received a letter from the City of Los Angeles notifying me that a photograph of my car, taken by a hidden camera two months ago, shows that I had driven through a red light. I don't remember driving my car through a red light. But I can't defend against the alleged vehicle code violation. I'll have to pay the $380 fine and go to Traffic School. That's correct, dear reader. The fine is $380. And another $35 for Traffic School.

Meanwhile, I go to the Cavendish West Club to cool off.

Partner and I reach Four Spades on the following hand.

The Bidding:

NORTH	EAST	SOUTH	WEST
—	—	1 ♣	Pass
1 ♡	Pass	1 ♠	Pass
4 ♠	Pass	Pass	Pass

North
- ♠ K Q 9 6
- ♡ Q J 10 6
- ◊ Q J 7
- ♣ 8 4

South
- ♠ J 10 8 7
- ♡ K 5 4
- ◊ A 8 3
- ♣ A Q 6

West leads the eight of hearts. I play dummy's queen, which holds, East encouraging with the nine.

From the play thus far, it's clear that my opponents are poised to win the first round of trumps and then play the ace and a heart, which West will ruff. I can pitch a diamond on dummy's fourth heart. At first sight, it appears I will need both the club and diamond finesses to make Four Spades.

But I see a chance to make Four Spades with only the club finesse working. If I eliminate the clubs before leading trumps and West holds only two trumps, then West will be endplayed after ruffing the heart. It's worth a try. And in any event, I must take the club finesse sometime.

I lead a club to the queen, which wins, and continue with the ace of clubs and a club ruff in dummy. Next, I lead the king of spades from dummy. West wins the ace and continues with a heart to East's ace. East returns a heart which West ruffs.

Fortunately, West is out of trumps. He is forced to lead a diamond from his king to dummy's queen-jack or give me a ruff and sluff with another club. West tries a diamond. I win dummy's queen, cash a high spade, and then pitch a diamond on dummy's queen of hearts, making Four Spades.

The complete hand:

North
♠ K Q 9 6
♡ Q J 10 6
◇ Q J 7
♣ 8 4

West
♠ A 5
♡ 8 3
◇ K 10 9 5 4
♣ J 9 7 2

East
♠ 4 3 2
♡ A 9 7 2
◇ 6 2
♣ K 10 5 3

South
♠ J 10 8 7
♡ K 5 4
◇ A 8 3
♣ A Q 6

West might defeat Four Spades by playing a club. Declarer ruffs in dummy, pitching a diamond from hand. Declarer must then guess whether to play dummy's high heart, which West might ruff, or take the diamond finesse. Declarer should, of course, play dummy's high heart, pitching a diamond from hand.

After the hand is over West informs me that at a recent National Tournament which he had attended, the A.C.B.L. had installed hidden cameras, "to detect and deter the cheating which occurs at duplicate bridge tournaments." West tells me that he likes the cameras because "there's a lot of cheating going on at bridge tournaments."

I have a different opinion. I hate hidden cameras. But who was I to disagree with the way the A.C.B.L. conducts its bridge tournaments?

I wonder if any of the hidden cameras were placed in bathrooms. And why not? After all, the A.C.B.L. contends that much of the cheating at bridge tournaments occurs in bathrooms.

The hidden cameras remind me of George Orwell's novel "1984". Be careful, dear reader. Big Brother is watching.

Hand 44

A SEX DATE

I'm taking my girl friend out to dinner tonight. But first I go to the Cavendish West Club for an afternoon of bridge. During the afternoon, I hold all the cards and win a ton of money. Then this hand comes along.

The Bidding:

NORTH	EAST	SOUTH	WEST
—	—	1 ♡	Pass
1 ♠	Pass	3 ♡	Pass
3 ♠	Pass	4 ♡	Pass
4NT	Pass	5 ♡	Pass
6 ♡	Pass	Pass	Pass

North
♠ A K 10 8 4 2
♡ J 3
◊ K Q
♣ K 7 4

South
♠ 5 3
♡ A K Q 10 9 8
◊ 6 5 4 3
♣ A

West leads the queen of clubs.

I have eleven top tricks, consisting of two spades, six hearts, one diamond and two clubs. At first glance, it appears right to win the ace of clubs, pull the missing trumps, and then play the ace and king of spades and ruff a spade. But the spades may be breaking four-one. If so, I won't be able to set up dummy's spades.

A better line of play would be to lead a spade to dummy's ace, pitch a spade on the king of clubs, ruff a spade, return to dummy with the jack of hearts, ruff another spade, and pull the trumps. Dummy's king-queen of diamonds would then provide an entry to the good spades. This line of play would succeed against a four-one spade break. But if both hearts and spades break four-one, Six Hearts would be set, for after ruffing two spades, I would be out of trumps. My opponents would then win the ace of diamonds and a club.

I see another line of play which appears best. At trick two, I lead a diamond to dummy's queen. If my opponents duck the queen of diamonds, I'll continue with a second diamond and later ruff a diamond in dummy for my twelfth trick.

East, however, refuses to make life easy by ducking the queen of diamonds. He wins the first diamond and returns a heart, which I win in hand with the ten. I enter dummy with a spade to the ace. Next, I cash dummy's king of clubs, pitching a spade from hand, and ruff a spade. West shows out on the second spade, East having started with four spades.

The rest is easy. I play a heart to dummy's jack, ruff another spade, and pull the remaining trumps. I then lead a diamond to dummy's king. Dummy's spades are high, so I make Six Hearts.

The complete hand:

North
♠ A K 10 8 4 2
♡ J 3
♢ K Q
♣ K 7 4

West
♠ 6
♡ 7 6 5 2
♢ 10 8 7
♣ Q J 10 3 2

East
♠ Q J 9 7
♡ 4
♢ A J 9 2
♣ 9 8 6 5

South
♠ 5 3
♡ A K Q 10 9 8
♢ 6 5 4 3
♣ A

Normally, our rubber bridge game lasts until 6 p.m. But today, I leave an hour early.

"Why are you leaving so early," asks East. "The game is good, and you're holding all the cards and winning all the money."

"I have to go," I reply with a grin on my face, "I have a sex date."

"Oh, really," says East, "Who is he?"

Hand 45

TOO MUCH BRIDGE

During my first semester of law school, one of my professors told the class that he expected a third of the first year students to drop out before the semester ended. He was correct. A third of the students found law school too difficult and dropped out. But studying law was easy for me, so easy in fact that I always had plenty of time to play bridge.

Playing rubber bridge, I deal myself one of my usual hands:

♠ 10 3 2   ♡ Q 8 7 3   ◇ J 8 5 4   ♣ 7 5

I Pass and West, on my left, opens the bidding with Three Clubs. Partner, sitting North, bids Four Clubs and East Passes. Things are looking up. Here I was, hoping that the opponents wouldn't bid a slam. Instead, partner appears to hold a powerhouse, probably enough to make a game our way.

I bid Four Hearts and West passes. Partner isn't done yet.

He raises me to Five Hearts and East Passes. Partner's Five Heart bid is a slam try. If I had two honors in hearts, I'd bid Six Hearts. But I have weak hearts, so I pass Five Hearts, which becomes the final contract.

The Bidding:

NORTH	EAST	SOUTH	WEST
—	—	Pass	3 ♣
4 ♣	Pass	4 ♡	Pass
5 ♡	Pass	Pass	Pass

West leads the king of clubs and partner puts down a hand which justifies his bidding:

North

♠ A K Q J 7 5

♡ A J 10 9

♢ A K

♣ 8

South

♠ 10 3 2

♡ Q 8 7 3

♢ J 8 5 4

♣ 7 5

Five Spades is a better contract than Five Hearts. But I don't blame partner for bidding Five Hearts. It was the only bid available to him to try for a slam.

The king of clubs holds and West continues with the queen of clubs, which I ruff in dummy. I have plenty of tricks. All I have to do to make Five Hearts is to limit my opponents to one trump trick.

I could lead a spade to hand and try the heart finesse. But from the bidding and play, West appears to hold six or seven clubs ace-king-queen. If West held the king of hearts as well, he probably would have opened the bidding with One Club, not Three Clubs. There's no use in taking the heart finesse. East is almost certain to hold the king of hearts.

I suppose I could play the ace of hearts and continue with a second heart from dummy. The problem with this line of play is that East may hold four hearts. If so, he'll duck the second heart. If I then play a third heart, East will win his king of hearts and play another club, forcing me to ruff with my last trump. No, playing the ace and another heart isn't the best play.

I see a way to handle a four-one heart split. At trick two, I lead the ten of hearts from dummy, which holds. I continue with the jack of hearts from dummy. If East ducks the jack of hearts, I'll continue with the ace of hearts and claim eleven tricks. But East wins the king of hearts and West shows out.

If East plays a club now, I will ruff in dummy with the ace of hearts, return to hand with the ten of spades, and draw East's remaining two trumps with my queen and eight of hearts. East tries a diamond instead. No matter. I win the diamond in dummy, cash the ace of hearts, return to hand with the ten of spades, and cash the queen of hearts, extracting East's last trump. Dummy is high now, so I make Five Hearts.

The complete hand:

North
♠ A K Q J 7 5
♡ A J 10 9
♢ A K
♣ 8

West
♠ 8 6
♡ 4
♢ 7 6 3
♣ A K Q 10 9 6 3

East
♠ 9 4
♡ K 6 5 2
♢ Q 10 9 2
♣ J 4 2

South
♠ 10 3 2
♡ Q 8 7 3
♢ J 8 5 4
♣ 7 5

I might have become a great attorney. Instead, after graduating law school, I played so much bridge that I never developed my legal skills beyond what was minimally necessary. That's what happens when you spend too much time playing bridge. Your career suffers.

Hand 46

TOO MUCH WORK

During the last month, I've put in 60 hours a week practicing law. I've been so busy as an attorney that I haven't been able to play any bridge whatsoever. But I'm taking the afternoon off today, for the first time in a month, to play some rubber bridge. And next month, I'm going to the Nationals for nine days of bridge and a well earned vacation.

Sitting West, I hold:

♠ 9 5   ♡ Q 10 8 4   ◇ A J 9 5   ♣ A Q 6

Partner, sitting East, opens the bidding with Two Hearts, weak. South, on my right, overcalls Two Spades. I bid Four Hearts and West, on my left, bids Four Spades. Partner and South Pass and it is my bid.

The obvious choices are Five Hearts, Double and Pass. Before choosing my next bid, I stop to consider several possible hands which partner may hold for his Two Heart bid.

On the auction, partner probably holds two spades. It's possible, though not likely, that partner has a singleton spade. Partner should hold one of these hands:

1. ♠ x x   ♡ A K x x x x   ◇ Q x x   ♣ x x

2. ♠ x x   ♡ A K J x x x   ◇ 10 x x   ♣ J x

3. ♠ x x   ♡ A K x x x x   ◇ Q x   ♣ x x x

4. ♠ x x   ♡ A K J x x x   ◇ x x   ♣ J x x

5. ♠ x   ♡ A K x x x x   ◇ Q x x   ♣ x x x

6. ♠ x   ♡ A K J x x x   ◇ x x x   ♣ J x x

On the first four hands, with partner holding two spades, Five Hearts is likely to go down one, and perhaps down two tricks. On the fifth and sixth hands, with partner holding a singleton spade, we'll need the club finesse to work and some luck in diamonds to make Five Hearts. In short, Five Hearts appears have very little chance of making. I expect that Five Hearts would be Doubled, for down one or down two.

What about our defensive chances? With any of these hands, we should be able to win a heart, two diamonds and a club, or a heart, a diamond and two clubs, and Four Spades should be down one. But I don't believe it likely that we can set Four Spades two tricks, so I'm not going to Double. I Pass Four Spades.

The Bidding:

NORTH	EAST	SOUTH	WEST
—	2 ♡	2 ♠	4 ♡
4 ♠	Pass	Pass	Pass

I lead a low heart and North puts down this dummy:

North
- ♠ Q 10 4 3
- ♡ 7
- ◇ K 7 6
- ♣ K 10 8 4 2

West
- ♠ 9 5
- ♡ Q 10 8 4
- ◇ A J 9 5
- ♣ A Q 6

Partner wins the king of hearts and returns the deuce of diamonds, showing three. South plays low and I insert the nine which forces dummy's king. Declarer leads a spade to hand, ruffs a heart in dummy, and continues with a second spade to hand. On the second spade, partner shows void, pitching a heart. Declarer then leads the three of clubs toward dummy's king-ten and it is my play.

Before deciding how to defend, I stop to count declarer's hand. To do so, I first count partner's hand. Partner began with a singleton spade, six hearts, three diamonds, and therefore three clubs. That gives South six spades, two hearts, three diamonds, and two clubs.

South holds one of these two hands:

1. ♠ A K J x x x ♡ x x ♢ x x x ♣ x x

2. ♠ A K J x x x ♡ x x ♢ Q x x ♣ x x

Since South cannot hold a singleton club, I can safely duck the club and let dummy win the king. But if I duck the club, declarer will win dummy's king of clubs and return a club to my queen. With the clubs breaking three-three, I would be forced to play the ace and another diamond. If partner holds the queen of diamonds, we'll set Four Spades. But if South holds the queen of diamonds, declarer will make Four Spades.

Winning the ace of clubs won't help either, for then I would be forced to play the ace and another diamond. If I were to win the ace of clubs and return a club, declarer would win dummy's king of clubs and ruff a club. With the clubs breaking three-three declarer would then enter dummy with a spade and pitch two diamonds on dummy's clubs. No, the ace of clubs isn't the right play either.

Instead of playing the ace of clubs or a low club, I play the queen of clubs, hoping to create an entry into partner's hand. If East holds the jack of clubs, East will be able to win the second club and lead another diamond for me.

Declarer wins the queen of clubs with the king and returns a low club from dummy. Fortunately, partner wins the second club with the nine. Partner returns a diamond through declarer's queen to my ace-jack, so Four Spades is down one.

The complete hand:

                          North
                          ♠ Q 10 4 3
                          ♡ 7
                          ◊ K 7 6
                          ♣ K 10 8 4 2

West   **East**
♠ 9 5   ♠ 6
♡ Q 10 8 4   ♡ A K J 9 3 2
◊ A J 9 5   ◊ 10 3 2
♣ A Q 6   ♣ J 9 5

                          South
                          ♠ A K J 8 7 2
                          ♡ 6 5
                          ◊ Q 8 4
                          ♣ 7 3

Four Spades cannot be set unless West plays the queen of clubs. This allows East to win the second club and lead a diamond through declarer's queen.

On this hand, East held the jack-nine of clubs over dummy's ten. East was therefore able to win the second club with the nine, without any discomfort. But if declarer held the nine of clubs doubleton, it would be necessary for East to rise with the jack of clubs after dummy won the king of clubs and led a low club.

One of my cases failed to settle and instead went to trial. As a result, I didn't get to play bridge at the Nationals as I had planned. My vacation consisted of a six day jury trial.

That's what happens when you spend too much time working. You miss out on all the fun you could have had playing bridge instead.

Hand 47

THE SPORTS BETTOR

People who play bridge for money often wager on other games. Some bet on golf. Others bet on gin rummy or pinochle. As for me, dear reader, I play bridge, poker, gin rummy and backgammon for money. And I also wager on professional football. But for sure, my best game is bridge.

Playing rubber bridge, I hold:

♠ A Q   ♡ K 7 6 4   ◇ 9 8 5   ♣ A K 4 3

I open the bidding with One No-Trump. West, on my left, Passes and partner, sitting North, raises me to Three No-Trump, which all Pass.

The Bidding:

NORTH	EAST	SOUTH	WEST
—	—	1NT	Pass
3NT	Pass	Pass	Pass

West leads the seven of spades. Partner puts down an excellent dummy:

North
♠ 6 4
♡ Q J 5
◇ A K J 10 7
♣ 6 5 2

South
♠ A Q
♡ K 7 6 4
◇ 9 8 5
♣ A K 4 3

East plays the jack of spades and I win the queen. I see three lines of play. The first line of play is to take the diamond finesse. If the diamond finesse wins, I will be able to win two spades, five diamonds, two clubs and at least two heart tricks. But if the diamond finesse loses, I will have only eight tricks, consisting of two spades, four diamonds and two clubs, and Three No-Trump will be set.

The second line of play is to play the hearts before playing the diamonds. If the hearts break three-three, I will have nine top tricks and I won't need the diamond finesse. And if the hearts break four-two, I can fall back on the diamond finesse. But the hearts may be breaking four-two and the diamond finesse may be off. If so, I still won't be able to win nine tricks.

The third and best line of play is to sneak home a heart trick and then play the diamonds. If West has the ace of hearts, I should lead a heart toward dummy's queen-jack, win a heart trick, and then play the diamonds. If West plays the ace of hearts, that will give me three tricks in hearts and I won't need the diamond finesse. But if East holds the ace of hearts, then I must lead a heart from dummy toward my king.

I must decide which of my opponents is more likely to hold the ace of hearts. There's nothing in the bidding to suggest which opponent is more likely to hold the ace of hearts. All I have to guide me is the opening lead.

West's seven of spades was fourth best. The missing spades under the seven are the five, three and deuce. West is almost certain to hold five, and perhaps six, spades. That gives East either three or four spades.

West has at least five spades, and therefore, he has at most eight cards outside of the spade suit. East, on the other hand, has either three or four spades. That gives East at least nine cards outside of the spade suit. Since East holds more cards outside of the spade suit than West, it's more likely that East, rather than West, will hold the ace of hearts.

I lead a diamond to dummy's ace and lead a low heart toward my king. East rises with the ace of hearts and returns a spade to my ace. I win the queen and jack of hearts in dummy, return to hand with the king of clubs and cash the king of hearts. I don't need to take the diamond finesse, so I cash the ace of clubs and the ace of diamonds and concede the last three tricks, making Three No-Trump.

The complete hand:

North
♠ 6 4
♡ Q J 5
♢ A K J 10 7
♣ 6 5 2

West
♠ K 10 8 7 5 2
♡ 9 2
♢ 6 2
♣ J 9 7

East
♠ J 9 3
♡ A 10 8 3
♢ Q 4 3
♣ Q 10 8

South
♠ A Q
♡ K 7 6 4
♢ 9 8 5
♣ A K 4 3

I have a great week at bridge and I win $1,200. Unfortunately, I lose $1,000 betting football. I wish I had the discipline to give up on betting sports. I'd be lot richer.

Hand 48

THE SLEEP DEPRIVED MAN

My right hand opponent is a fine bridge player. He tells me that he's played rubber bridge continuously since yesterday afternoon. He must be exhausted. But rather than go home and get some sleep, he's decided to play on.

Sitting South, I deal myself the following hand:

♠ A Q 9 7 3   ♡ K 9 3   ◇ K J 4   ♣ A 5

I open the bidding with One Spade. West Passes and partner raises me to Three Spades, a limit raise, and East Passes. I bid Four Spades and all Pass.

The Bidding:

NORTH	EAST	SOUTH	WEST
—	—	1 ♠	Pass
3 ♠	Pass	4 ♠	Pass
Pass	Pass		

West leads the queen of clubs and partner puts down this dummy:

North
♠ K J 10 8 2
♡ 6 2
◇ A 7 6
♣ 9 3 2

South
♠ A Q 9 7 3
♡ K 9 3
◇ K J 4
♣ A 5

I play a low club from dummy and East plays the eight. There may be some advantage in allowing West to win the club, so I play low. West continues with the jack of clubs, which I win with the ace. Four Spades can be made if East holds either the ace of hearts or the queen of diamonds. If West holds both the ace of hearts and the queen of diamonds, I will probably lose two hearts and a diamond, for down one.

After winning the ace of clubs, I lead a spade to dummy and ruff dummy's last club. I then lead a second spade to dummy. The spades break two-one, East showing void on the second round.

The normal play at this point is to cash the ace of diamonds and finesse the jack of diamonds. This gains when West holds the queen of diamonds doubleton, for after winning the queen of diamonds, West would be endplayed. And if West wins the queen of diamonds and returns a diamond, I can still make Four Spades if East holds the ace of hearts.

But I see another line of play, based upon East being caught off guard. I lead a heart from dummy toward my king-nine. If East fails to play an honor, I can guarantee making Four Spades by playing the nine of hearts.

Sure enough, when I lead a heart from dummy East plays low. I play the nine of hearts and West wins the jack. No matter how West continues, I must win ten tricks. If West leads a heart, then my king of hearts will be good for a diamond pitch from dummy. And if West leads a diamond, it will be into my king-jack.

The complete hand:

North
♠ K J 10 8 2
♡ 6 2
◇ A 7 6
♣ 9 3 2

West
♠ 6 4
♡ A J 7 4
◇ Q 8 2
♣ Q J 10 6

East
♠ 5
♡ Q 10 8 5
◇ 10 9 5 3
♣ K 8 7 4

South
♠ A Q 9 7 3
♡ K 9 3
◇ K J 4
♣ A 5

East slipped in the defense. East should play the ten of hearts on the first heart from dummy. Declarer covers the ten of hearts with the king and West wins the ace. West returns a heart to East's queen. East then shifts to the ten of diamonds, declarer finesses, and Four Spades is down one.

East is a fine bridge player. Ordinarily, he would have found this defense. But East had gone too long without any sleep. That's what happens when you play bridge for too many hours. You lose the ability to play your best game.

Hand 49

THE SPONSOR

In bridge tournaments, wealthy players often hire experts to play with them. The experts then play with the sponsor and considerably improve the sponsor's chances of winning an event.

My partner in a team of four event has limited skills. He's hired me and two other experts to play on his team.

Sitting South, I hold:

♠ A K J 9   ♡ A 5 4   ◇ J 7 3   ♣ K 6 5

I open the bidding with One No-Trump. West, on my left, Passes. Partner, sitting North, bids Two Hearts, as a transfer to Two Spades. I bid Two Spades, West Passes again, and partner bids Three No-Trump. East Passes and I bid Four Spades, which all Pass.

The Bidding:

NORTH	EAST	SOUTH	WEST
—	—	1NT	Pass
2 ♡*	Pass	2 ♠	Pass
3NT	Pass	4 ♠	Pass
Pass	Pass		

*transfer

West leads the four of spades and North puts down this dummy:

North
♠ Q 10 8 7 6
♡ K 7 2
◇ A K
♣ 8 3 2

South
♠ A K J 9
♡ A 5 4
◇ J 7 3
♣ K 6 5

I win the ace and king of spades in hand. The spades break two-two. I have nine top tricks consisting of five spades, two hearts, and two diamonds. Unless the queen of diamonds is doubleton, it will be necessary to win a trick with the king of clubs to make Four Spades.

Unfortunately, West's trump lead suggests that he holds high cards in the side suits. It's likely, therefore, that West holds the ace of clubs. I must devise a line of play which will allow me to make Four Spades when West holds the ace of clubs.

I see two lines of play. The first line of play is to cash the ace and king of diamonds, the ace and king of hearts, ruff a diamond in dummy and then play another heart. If West holds five hearts, or the queen of hearts third and fails to unblock, West will be forced to win the third heart and he will be endplayed.

This line of play will also succeed if West holds the ace of clubs doubleton, for if East wins the third heart and leads a club, I can duck the first club and then play the king of clubs. When West wins the ace of clubs, he will be out of clubs and forced to play a heart of a diamond which I can ruff in dummy, pitching a club from hand.

The second line of play is to play the ace and king of diamonds, the king and ace of hearts, and then play the jack of diamonds, pitching a heart from dummy. This line of play succeeds when West holds the queen of diamonds and a doubleton heart. Upon winning the jack of diamonds, West will be endplayed.

Which is the better line of play? The first line of play is obviously better. All that it requires is for West to hold five hearts. The second line of play requires West to hold the queen of diamonds and a doubleton heart. For the moment, I adopt the first line of play.

I begin by selecting a sequence of play which is least likely to alert West to the need to unblock his heart queen. I play a heart to dummy's king, then play the ace and king of diamonds and a heart to my ace. West plays the eight and jack of hearts under the ace and king.

The missing hearts are the queen, ten and nine. If West had five hearts queen-jack-ten, he surely would have led the queen of hearts rather than a spade. I'm sure that West does not hold five hearts. But it's possible that West holds a doubleton jack of hearts. In short, I'm going to switch my game plan.

I play the jack of diamonds from hand, hoping that West will cover with the queen. Sure enough, West plays the queen of diamonds. This does me no harm. I pitch a low heart from dummy. If West began with a doubleton heart, he'll be endplayed.

West, however, has another heart to lead. He leads the queen of hearts. Instead of ruffing, I pitch a club from dummy. West is forced to lead a club now from his ace-queen to my king, or give me a sluff and a ruff, so I make Four Spades.

The complete hand:

North
♠ Q 10 8 7 6
♡ K 7 2
◇ A K
♣ 8 3 2

West
♠ 4 3
♡ Q J 8
◇ Q 10 8 4
♣ A Q 9 7

East
♠ 5 2
♡ 10 9 6 3
◇ 9 6 5 2
♣ J 10 4

South
♠ A K J 9
♡ A 5 4
◇ J 7 3
♣ K 6 5

Four Spades can be set. To set Four Spades, West must unblock the queen and jack of hearts under the ace and king. This allows East to win the third heart and shift to the jack of clubs through declarer's king.

With our beefed up team, we manage to win eight matches and we place first overall. Our sponsor is delighted. After the tournament is over, he gives each of us a check for our services, plus a generous bonus for placing first overall.

Hand 50

A CHOICE OF FINESSES

After working all week, most Americans relax on the weekends. Some go to movies or watch television. Others play golf. And me? I spend most of my leisure time playing bridge.

Playing rubber bridge, I hold the following hand as South:

♠ A J 10 7 5   ♡ 10 2   ♢ A Q 6 2   ♣ A 9

North and East pass and I open the bidding with One Spade. West overcalls Two Clubs and partner raises me to Three Spades. East passes and I bid Four Spades, which ends the auction.

The Bidding:

NORTH	EAST	SOUTH	WEST
Pass	Pass	1 ♠	2 ♣
3 ♠	Pass	4 ♠	Pass
Pass	Pass		

West leads the king of clubs and partner puts down this dummy:

North
♠ Q 9 8 6
♡ A Q J 9 3
♢ 5 4
♣ 7 2

South
♠ A J 10 7 5
♡ 10 2
♢ A Q 6 2
♣ A 9

For the moment, I duck the king of clubs. This prevents East from winning the second club and shifting to a diamond. West continues with the queen of clubs, which I win with the ace.

With normal breaks, Four Spades will fail only if the spade, heart and diamond finesses lose. I should be able to pitch all of my diamond losers on dummy's hearts, so I don't need the diamond finesse to work. All I need to do to make Four Spades is to prevent my opponents from winning a diamond trick before I pull trumps and set up the hearts.

I could play the ace and jack of spades, but then East might win the king of spades and shift to a diamond. No, that won't do. I could also try the heart finesse now, but then East might win the king of hearts and shift to a diamond. No, that won't do either.

I don't think I need to finesse the hearts. If West holds the king of hearts, I should be able to make Four Spades by taking the spade finesse early and setting up the hearts later.

I lead a low heart to dummy's ace, giving up on the heart finesse. I then lead the nine of spades which West wins with the king. West desperately shifts to a diamond, but I win with the queen. I pull the remaining trumps and concede a heart to East's king, making Four Spades.

The complete hand:

North
♠ Q 9 8 6
♡ A Q J 9 3
◇ 5 4
♣ 7 2

West
♠ K 4
♡ 7 5 4
◇ K 9 7
♣ K Q J 8 3

East
♠ 3 2
♡ K 8 6
◇ J 10 8 3
♣ 10 6 5 4

South
♠ A J 10 7 5
♡ 10 2
◇ A Q 6 2
♣ A 9

If declarer takes the heart finesse, East wins the king of hearts and shifts to the jack of diamonds and Four Spades is down one.

After a heart to the ace and the losing spade finesse, Four Spades can be set only if West is able to play the king and another heart for East to ruff and the diamond finesse is off.

Of course, West might have led a heart to East's king. After a third heart from East, declarer must guess whether to pitch a diamond and risk a ruff, or ruff the heart and take the diamond finesse. Fortunately, I wasn't put to this guess.

Hand 51

THE ANTIQUE

During the years 1962-1964, I lived in New York. I had a job for a while, but I soon discovered that I could make more money playing rubber bridge than I could earn working. I played bridge every day. Some of the clubs were open day and night. As a result, I often played bridge for more than twenty-four hours, nonstop.

Now, more than forty years later, I still play rubber bridge whenever I can. Sitting South I hold:

♠ A K 10 9 7 3   ♡ 8 2   ◇ 10 7 3   ♣ 5 2

Partner and I bid to Four Spades on this auction:

The Bidding:

NORTH	EAST	SOUTH	WEST
1 ♣	Pass	1 ♠	Pass
2 ◇	Pass	2 ♠	Pass
2NT	Pass	3 ♠	Pass
4 ♠	Pass	Pass	Pass

West leads the king of hearts and partner puts down this dummy:

North
♠ 5
♡ A J 7
◇ A K 8 4
♣ A J 7 6 3

South
♠ A K 10 9 7 3
♡ 8 2
◇ 10 7 3
♣ 5 2

The opening lead is very favorable. With any luck, I should be able to win five tricks in spades, two hearts, two diamonds, and a club for a total of ten tricks.

I don't see any advantage in ducking the king of hearts, so I win the ace of hearts in dummy. I then lead a spade to my ace and king, pitching a low club from dummy. East plays low on the first spade, but on the second spade he drops the jack.

The missing spades are the queen and the eight, and West may well hold both spades. I can't afford to lead the ten of spades now, for I need to set up the jack of hearts for a pitch. I therefore lead a heart toward dummy's jack.

West wins the queen of hearts and shifts to the ten of clubs which I win with dummy's ace, East dropping the nine. From the play of the clubs, West probably holds the doubleton ten and East the king-queen fourth. I cash dummy's jack of hearts, pitching a club, as both opponents follow.

It appears best at this point to ruff a club back to hand and then play the ten of spades. But if West holds the queen-eight of spades, he will win the ten of spades and shift to a diamond which I will be forced to win in dummy.

It would then be impossible for me to exit dummy without allowing East to win the lead. And if East wins the lead, he will play a high club which will promote West's eight of spades into the setting trick.

I see a chance to thwart this defense. Before ruffing a club to hand, I cash dummy's ace and king of diamonds. If I'm lucky, West will hold only two diamonds and West won't be able to stick me in dummy later.

After cashing the diamonds, I ruff a club back to hand and lead the ten of spades. West wins the queen of spades, East showing void. Fortunately, West is out of diamonds. West plays a heart, which I ruff low. I then cash the nine of spades, extracting West's last trump, and later concede a diamond to East, making Four Spades.

The complete hand:

North
♠ 5
♡ A J 7
♢ A K 8 4
♣ A J 7 6 3

West
♠ Q 8 6 2
♡ K Q 10 9 4
♢ 9 2
♣ 10 4

East
♠ J 4
♡ 6 5 3
♢ Q J 6 5
♣ K Q 9 8

South
♠ A K 10 9 7 3
♡ 8 2
♢ 10 7 3
♣ 5 2

At the time declarer played the ace and king of diamonds, it appeared that West held four spades and a doubleton club. West's remaining cards were likely to be five hearts and two diamonds or four hearts and three diamonds. With either of these likely distributions, West would be unable to ruff a diamond. Hence, there was little risk in playing the ace and king of diamonds and much to be gained.

Much has happened since I lived in New York. I've gained thirty pounds and my hair has turned grey. And I no longer have the stamina to play twenty-four hours of bridge. My age, waist line and IQ are converging at room temperature levels. I've become an antique. I wish I were fifty again.

Hand 52

PERCENTAGE PLAY

Playing rubber bridge, partner and I bid to Six Spades on the following hand:

The Bidding:

NORTH	EAST	SOUTH	WEST
—	—	1NT	Pass
2 ♣	Pass	2 ♠	Pass
6 ♠	Pass	Pass	Pass

North
♠ A K J 8
♡ 7 6
◊ 5 2
♣ A K 8 3 2

South
♠ Q 10 9 7
♡ A 8
◊ A K Q 7
♣ J 5 4

West leads the king of hearts:

Six Spades is an excellent contract. With the diamonds available for a heart pitch, I can make Six Spades so long as both spades and clubs break three two.

I win the ace of hearts and play the ace and king of spades. East and West follow suit. I continue with another trump to my queen, extracting the last trump. East shows void, pitching a heart, as West follows.

Next, I play the ace, king and queen of diamonds, pitching dummy's losing heart. East shows void on the second diamond, West having started with six diamonds.

The normal play at this point is the ace and king of clubs. With this line of play, I can make Six Spades if the clubs break three-two or the queen of clubs is singleton. But I don't think the clubs are going to break three-two.

West began with three spades, the king-queen of hearts, and six diamonds. That gives him two unknown cards. With seven missing hearts and five missing clubs, West is far more likely to hold a heart and a club rather than two clubs.

A good method to follow to estimate the likelihood of a four-one club split is to count the possible combinations of the hearts and clubs in the West hand. There are seven hearts other than the king and queen and there are five missing clubs. That makes thirty-five different ways for West to hold the king-queen third of hearts and a singleton club (7 times 5).

If West holds the king-queen of hearts doubleton, then West would hold two of the five missing clubs. There are ten different ways for West to hold two clubs (5 times 4, divided by 2). The approximate odds in favor of a four-one club split are therefore 35 to 10.

If the clubs are four-one, as I suspect, then West will hold one of the following hands:

1. ♠ x x x   ♡ K Q x   ◊ J 10 x x x x   ♣ x

2. ♠ x x x   ♡ K Q x   ◊ J 10 x x x x   ♣ Q

Unless West holds the queen of clubs singleton, the normal play of the ace and king of clubs won't work. East will win the third club with the queen and return a heart, which I will ruff in dummy. Since dummy's clubs wouldn't be high, I would be forced to ruff a club to hand and concede a diamond to West, for down one.

What if I lead a club to dummy's king and return a club toward my jack? No, that won't work either. East would win the queen of clubs and return a heart, which dummy would ruff. Even though the jack of clubs would be high, the clubs would be blocked.

With the clubs blocked, if I were to cash the jack of clubs, I would have no entry to dummy's ace of clubs. And if I were to overtake the jack of clubs with dummy's ace, then East's ten of clubs would be high.

But there is a way to make Six Spades. I ruff a heart in dummy and lead a low club from dummy's ace-king toward my jack. If West holds the queen of clubs, he will win the queen and cash a diamond.

But if East holds the queen of clubs, I will make Six Spades.

Fortunately, East holds the queen of clubs. East wins the queen of clubs, but he has no diamonds. East returns a heart, which I ruff in hand. I then cash the jack of clubs and continue with the ace and king of clubs, so I make Six Spades.

The complete hand:

North
♠ A K J 8
♡ 7 6
◇ 5 2
♣ A K 8 3 2

West
♠ 6 5 3
♡ K Q 10
◇ J 10 8 6 4 3
♣ 7

East
♠ 4 2
♡ J 9 5 4 3 2
◇ 9
♣ Q 10 9 6

South
♠ Q 10 9 7
♡ A 8
◇ A K Q 7
♣ J 5 4

Once in a while, when you make an unusual play like this one, West holds the queen of clubs singleton and you go down on a hand that everyone else would make. But if the clubs are divided four-one, leading a club toward your jack wins eighty percent of the time while the alternative play of the ace of clubs wins only twenty percent of the time.

Hand 53

A WILD RIDE

I lost $2,000 this week playing poker. I also lost $800 at gin rummy and another $500 playing rubber bridge. But I'm still well ahead on the week. I won over $4,000 in one day, playing in the biggest gambling game ever invented. I'll tell you about that game later, dear reader.

Meanwhile, playing rubber bridge, I hold the following hand as East:

♠ A K Q 3   ♡ Q J 3   ◇ K J 6 5   ♣ 9 4

North, on my right, opens the bidding with One Heart. I could overcall One No-Trump, but we might miss a spade fit, so I Double instead. South, on my left, Redoubles, showing a good hand. Partner, sitting West, bids One Spade. North bids Two Hearts and I bid Two Spades. South jumps to Five Clubs, which all Pass.

The Bidding:

NORTH	EAST	SOUTH	WEST
1 ♡	Dbl	Rdbl	1 ♠
2 ♡	2 ♠	5 ♣	Pass
Pass	Pass		

Partner leads the deuce of spades, showing four, and North puts down this dummy:

North
♠ 7 4
♡ A K 10 9 6 5
◊ A 10 4 2
♣ 6

East
♠ A K Q 3
♡ Q J 3
◊ K J 6 5
♣ 9 4

I win the queen of spades and declarer plays low. It's time now to consider declarer's hand and how best to defend against Five Clubs.

For his five club bid, declarer ought to hold seven solid clubs. South's other cards ought to be three spades, a heart and two diamonds or three spades, two hearts and one diamond. South should hold one of the following hands:

1. ♠ x x x   ♡ x   ◊ x x   ♣ A K Q J x x x

2. ♠ x x x   ♡ x x   ◊ x   ♣ A K Q J x x x

I could cash another spade and then shift to a trump. But declarer would cash three rounds of trumps and then play a heart to dummy's ace and king and ruff a heart. With the hearts breaking, declarer would make Five Clubs. No, passive defense won't set Five Clubs.

The ace of diamonds is the entry to the hearts. To set five clubs, I must return a diamond to knock out dummy's ace. Since declarer may hold the singleton queen of diamonds, I return the king of diamonds. Sure enough, South holds the queen of diamonds singleton. The king of diamonds knocks out dummy's ace. No matter how declarer continues, Five Clubs is down one.

The complete hand:

North
♠ 7 4
♡ A K 10 9 6 5
◊ A 10 4 2
♣ 6

West
♠ J 8 5 2
♡ 8 7
◊ 9 8 7 3
♣ 8 3 2

East
♠ A K Q 3
♡ Q J 3
◊ K J 6 5
♣ 9 4

South
♠ 10 9 6
♡ 4 2
◊ Q
♣ A K Q J 10 7 5

Even though West has four spades, he should not bid over the Redouble. The best way to show a weak hand is to Pass. By bidding One Spade freely, West suggests a better hand.

If South held a doubleton diamond and a singleton heart, it would still be necessary for East to play the king of diamonds, to knock out dummy's ace. Five Clubs would still be down one, provided West held the queen of diamonds. If South held a singleton heart and the doubleton queen of diamonds, no defense would set Five Clubs.

Earlier, dear reader, I promised to tell you about a big gambling game. I won my $4,000 playing in the biggest gambling game ever invented, stock options. I bought some Microsoft calls for $3,370. Microsoft went up several points and I sold my options the same day for $7,490. After commissions, I made over $4,000.

If you really want to gamble for high stakes, try buying some options on IBM, Intel, Microsoft, Ebay or Google. I promise you a wild ride.

Hand 54

TEST YOUR DEFENSE

North
♠ 10 8 3
♡ K 7 6 3
◇ A Q J 8
♣ J 2

East
♠ Q 2
♡ 4
◇ 9 6 5 3
♣ A K 10 7 6 3

NORTH	EAST	SOUTH	WEST
Pass	Pass	1 ♠	Pass
3 ♠	Pass	4 ♠	Pass
Pass	Pass		

Playing rubber bridge, with both sides vulnerable, you find yourself defending Four Spades against a competent declarer.

West leads the queen of hearts which South wins in hand with the ace. Declarer cashes the ace of spades and continues with the king, jack, and ace of diamonds. Partner ruffs the third diamond with the king of spades.

West continues with the jack of hearts, dummy plays the king, and you ruff. How should you continue?

It's natural at this point to play the ace and king of clubs. If declarer has two clubs, you will set Four Spades. But is declarer likely to hold two clubs?

South began with six spades and three diamonds. His other cards should be either two clubs and two hearts or a singleton club and three hearts.

If South's distribution were 6-2-3-2, his correct play earlier would have been to play the ace and another spade or double finesse the spades. With a distribution of 6-2-3-2, declarer's actual play would fail whenever the diamonds split four-two or five-one.

Declarer's play makes sense only if his distribution is 6-3-3-1. With 6-3-3-1, a four-two diamond split wouldn't hurt. Only an uneven break in diamonds coupled with an unlikely five-one heart split could set Four Spades.

Since declarer's distribution is almost certain to be 6-3-3-1, the correct play is to underlead the ace-king of clubs to partner's queen so that partner can cash the ten of hearts.

The complete hand:

North
- ♠ 10 8 3
- ♡ K 7 6 3
- ◊ A Q J 8
- ♣ J 2

West
- ♠ K 7
- ♡ Q J 10 8 2
- ◊ 10 4
- ♣ Q 9 8 4

East
- ♠ Q 2
- ♡ 4
- ◊ 9 6 5 3
- ♣ A K 10 7 6 3

South
- ♠ A J 9 6 5 4
- ♡ A 9 5
- ◊ K 7 2
- ♣ 5

Hand 55

A CURIOUS HAND

Playing rubber bridge, I hold:

♠ A Q 9   ♡ A J 5 2   ◇ A Q 6   ♣ A Q 7

Sitting South, I open the bidding with Two Clubs, strong. West Passes and partner responds Two Diamonds, weak. I rebid Two No-Trump and North bids Three Hearts, transfer to Three Spades. I should have a good play for game with any hand partner holds, so I bid Four Spades. North raises me to Six Spades, which all Pass.

The Bidding:

NORTH	EAST	SOUTH	WEST
Pass	Pass	2 ♣	Pass
2 ◇	Pass	2NT	Pass
3 ♡**	Pass	4 ♠	Pass
6 ♠	Pass	Pass	Pass
**transfer			

West leads a spade, North puts down this dummy:

North
♠ K J 10 8 7
♡ 8
◇ K 8 4 2
♣ 10 9 2

South
♠ A Q 9
♡ A J 5 2
◇ A Q 6
♣ A Q 7

I can count ten top tricks consisting of five spades, a heart, three diamonds and a club. I can gain an extra trick with a dummy reversal, by ruffing three hearts in dummy. That's eleven tricks. I should be able to win a twelfth trick with a three-three diamond break, a club finesse, or an endplay.

I win the first spade in hand, cash the ace of hearts, and ruff a heart in dummy. I don't want an opponent to pitch a diamond when I ruff the fourth heart, so I shall return to hand with diamonds, saving a trump entry for later.

I continue with a diamond to the ace and another heart ruff in dummy. I then lead a diamond to my queen and ruff my last heart in dummy. The hearts break four-four, so there are no more hearts in play. I then play a spade to my ace and queen. The spades break three-two, West having started with three spades.

At this point, with the spades breaking three-two and the hearts breaking four-four, Six Spades is cold against any distribution. But to guarantee the contract, I must discard the *ten of clubs* from dummy.

I lead a diamond to dummy's king. If the diamonds break three-three, I will cash the last diamond. And if West holds four diamonds, then a diamond from dummy will endplay West, forcing him to lead into my ace-queen of clubs.

As it turns out, East holds four diamonds. No matter, I lead the nine of clubs from dummy. If East plays low, I will duck, allowing West to win the jack. West will then be endplayed, forced to lead a club into my ace-queen.

East, however, covers the nine of clubs with the jack, I play the queen, and West wins the king. This leaves West on play with the 8-6 of clubs to lead into my A-7, so I make Six Spades.

The complete hand:

North
♠ K J 10 8 7
♡ 8
♢ K 8 4 2
♣ 10 9 2

West
♠ 6 5 2
♡ K 9 6 4
♢ 5 3
♣ K 8 6 5

East
♠ 4 3
♡ Q 10 7 3
♢ J 10 9 7
♣ J 4 3

South
♠ A Q 9
♡ A J 5 2
♢ A Q 6
♣ A Q 7

If North discards a low club, rather than the ten, this places the contract in jeopardy. After cashing the king of diamonds, North leads the ten of clubs from dummy's 10-9. If East covers with the jack, South has a difficult guess.

If East has the king-jack of clubs, then South must finesse the queen of clubs. But if South finesses the queen of clubs and West wins the king, then a club return leaves North with a losing diamond. And if South overtakes dummy's nine of clubs with the ace, then West's eight of clubs will win the last trick.

If South wins the jack of clubs with the ace and returns a club, then East might win the king of clubs and the high diamond. That's why it's necessary to discard ten of clubs from dummy on the queen of spades.

Hand 56

THE MAN OF STEEL

In the mornings, I enter my office as a mild mannered attorney. At the end of the day, I go to my condo, change my clothes, and emerge as the bridge playing Man of Steel. Join me now, dear reader, for another thrilling adventure with the bridge playing Man of Steel.

The Bidding:

NORTH	EAST	SOUTH	WEST
—	—	—	4 ♡
Pass	Pass	4 ♠	Pass
Pass	Pass		

North
- ♠ 6 5 3
- ♡ 8 6 3
- ◊ 10 7 6 2
- ♣ A 9 4

South
- ♠ A K Q J 9
- ♡ 5 2
- ◊ A K
- ♣ Q 8 7 5

Against Four Spades West leads the ace, king and queen of hearts. East discards a diamond on the third heart and I ruff. East's discard must be from five or six diamonds.

I have five tricks in spades and two tricks in diamonds. To make Four Spades, I must win three tricks in clubs.

There are several possible lines of play to win three club tricks. The first, and most likely, is to find the clubs split three-three, with East holding the king of clubs.

A second line of play to win three club tricks is to find West with the doubleton king of clubs. If West holds the king of clubs doubleton, I could win three tricks in clubs by leading a club to dummy's nine, which East would win with the ten. I would later play a club to dummy's ace, picking up West's king, and then finesse the eight of clubs against East's jack.

A third line of play to win three club tricks is to play the ace of clubs. If West holds the king of clubs singleton, or if either opponent holds the jack-ten of clubs doubleton, I could win three tricks in clubs.

I'll decide later how to play the clubs. First, I play three rounds of trumps. West follows to all three rounds. East discards another diamond on the third round of spades. Since West followed to the spades, West began with three spades and six hearts. That leaves West with four unknown cards.

I cash the ace and king of diamonds to discover West's distribution. West follows to both diamonds, which means that West's distribution is 3-6-2-2. Since West holds only two clubs, I must play him for a doubleton king of clubs.

I lead a club to dummy's nine, which East wins with the ten. East returns a club, I play low, West the king and dummy wins the ace. I then finesse the eight of clubs, making Four Spades.

The complete hand:

                        North
                        ♠ 6 5 3
                        ♡ 8 6 3
                        ◊ 10 7 6 2
                        ♣ A 9 4

West   **East**
♠ 10 8 2   ♠ 7 4
♡ A K Q J 10 4   ♡ 9 7
◊ 4 3   ◊ Q J 9 8 5
♣ K 3   ♣ J 10 6 2

                        South
                        ♠ A K Q J 9
                        ♡ 5 2
                        ◊ A K
                        ♣ Q 8 7 5

"You sure were lucky to make Four Spades," says East. I have to agree.

Hand 57

AN AMAZING FEAT

This is a curious hand in which declarer is in jeopardy of losing a trump trick even though the trumps held by the combined hands consist of the A-K-Q-J-10-9-7-5.

Sitting South, I hold:

♠ K 10 7 5   ♡ K 6   ♢ A Q 8 7   ♣ A K Q

I open the bidding with Two No-Trump. West Passes and North bids Three Clubs, Stayman. East Passes and I respond Three Spades. North jumps to Four No-Trump, Blackwood, and I respond Five Hearts, showing two aces. Partner then bids Six Spades, which all Pass.

The Bidding:

NORTH	EAST	SOUTH	WEST
—	—	2NT	Pass
3 ♣	Pass	3 ♠	Pass
4NT	Pass	5 ♡	Pass
6 ♠	Pass	Pass	Pass

West leads a spade and North puts down this dummy:

North
♠ A Q J 9
♡ Q 9 7 4 2
♢ 6
♣ J 9 7

South
♠ K 10 7 5
♡ K 6
♢ A Q 8 7
♣ A K Q

Too bad West led a trump. Without a trump lead, I would have sufficient entries to ruff two hearts in hand and I could make Six Spades with either a three-three or four-two heart split. With a trump lead, however, I can't set up dummy's hearts unless they break three-three.

I have the entries to ruff three diamonds in dummy. Ruffing three diamonds in dummy appears to be better than playing to set up dummy's hearts. I therefore win the queen of spades in dummy and continue with the ace of diamonds and a diamond ruff, a club to hand and another diamond ruff in dummy.

On the third round of diamonds East pitches a club, West having started with six diamonds. I lead another club to hand and ruff my last diamond in dummy, East pitching another club. This is the position after I ruff my last diamond in dummy:

North
♠ —
♡ Q 9 7 4 2
◊ —
♣ J

West
♠ 8 3
♡ A 3
◊ K J
♣ —

East
♠ 6
♡ J 10 8 5
◊ —
♣ 8

South
♠ K 10 7
♡ K 6
◊ —
♣ Q

There is only one club left in play. I can't exit dummy with a club, for the club would be ruffed. Instead, I lead a heart to my king. West wins the ace of hearts and returns a heart to dummy's queen. I ruff the third round of hearts with the seven of spades, but West overruffs with the eight of spades, so I am down one in Six Spades, having accomplished the amazing feat of losing a trump trick to West's eight of spades.

The complete hand:

North
♠ A Q J 9
♡ Q 9 7 4 2
♢ 6
♣ J 9 7

West
♠ 8 3 2
♡ A 3
♢ K J 10 9 5 2
♣ 10 4

East
♠ 6 4
♡ J 10 8 5
♢ 4 3
♣ 8 6 5 3 2

South
♠ K 10 7 5
♡ K 6
♢ A Q 8 7
♣ A K Q

Six Spades can be made. After ruffing my last diamond, I should have led the queen of hearts from dummy rather than a low heart to my king. If I had led the queen of hearts, West could not have prevented me from returning to hand and pulling the remaining trumps.

If there's any insight to be gained from this hand, it is this: Some bridge authors write a better game of bridge than they play.

Hand 58

THE DENTIST

Occasionally, one of the players in our bridge game is quite nasty. When this happens, he makes the game miserable for everyone.

Tonight, West is the culprit. He's a dentist and he can well afford his losses. But he's in a bad mood because he's losing. The dentist lets me make a game that should have been set. He then tells me that he'd like to perform some root canal surgery on me, without an anesthetic.

On the next hand, I hold the following as South:

♠ K 3   ♡ Q J 10 8 3   ♢ A J 8 3   ♣ 8 4

I open the bidding with One Heart. It's a light opener, but it's better to open light rather than Pass and compete later. The dentist, on my left, overcalls Two Spades, weak. Partner, sitting North, bids a cheerful Three Diamonds and East jams the bidding with Four Spades.

No doubt East has a weak hand with four or five spades. My king of spades is surely facing a singleton or a void. Even though I have four card support for partner's suit, I don't want to encourage partner with the worthless king of spades in my hand, so I Pass. West Passes and partner comes to life with Six Hearts. This is passed around to West who bellows a loud Double, which all Pass.

The Bidding:

NORTH	EAST	SOUTH	WEST
—	—	1 ♡	2 ♠
3 ◇	4 ♠	Pass	Pass
6 ♡	Pass	Pass	Dbl
Pass	Pass	Pass	

West leads the queen of spades. Partner puts down an excellent dummy for me:

North
♠ A
♡ K 9 5
◊ K Q 10 9 6 5
♣ A K 7

South
♠ K 3
♡ Q J 10 8 3
◊ A J 8 3
♣ 8 4

West must hold the ace of hearts for his Double. It's possible that West holds four hearts. No doubt, all the suits will be breaking badly. There should be several singletons in play.

I win the ace of spades in dummy and continue with the king of hearts, which is allowed to hold the trick. I then lead a second heart to my ten, which also holds. East shows void on the second heart, pitching a low spade.

It looks correct now to lead another heart to West's ace. But then West might win the heart and lead a club. This would force me to guess how to exit dummy.

Before leading a third heart, I stop to consider West's distribution. For his Two Spade bid, West ought to hold six spades. He also holds four hearts. West should therefore hold one of the following hands:

1. ♠ Q J 10 x x x   ♡ A x x x ◊ x x x ♣ —

2. ♠ Q J 10 x x x   ♡ A x x x ◊ x x   ♣ x

3. ♠ Q J 10 x x x   ♡ A x x x ◊ x   ♣ x x

4. ♠ Q J 10 x x x   ♡ A x x x ◊ —   ♣ x x x

I don't think West holds the first hand, for it's unlikely that East would be void in diamonds and also have a singleton heart. And with a diamond void, East probably would have doubled Six Hearts, to ask for an unusual lead.

If West holds the second hand, then it will be necessary for me to win the club and return to hand with a diamond. If I were to attempt to exit dummy by playing a second club and ruffing a club, West would ruff the second club and Six Hearts would be down one.

It won't matter what I do if West holds the third hand. I could exit dummy safely with clubs or diamonds. But if West holds the fourth hand, it will be necessary for me to win the club in dummy and continue with a second club. If I were to try to exit dummy by playing a diamond to my ace, West would ruff.

I see a way to avert a later guess about how to exit dummy safely. Before playing a third heart, I cash dummy's ace of clubs. West follows to the club, so Six Hearts is cold now. I play a third heart to West's ace. No matter how West continues, I can return to hand, draw West's last trump and claim twelve tricks.

The complete hand:

North
♠ A
♡ K 9 5
◊ K Q 10 9 6 5
♣ A K 7

West
♠ Q J 10 7 5 2
♡ A 7 4 2
◊ 4 2
♣ 9

East
♠ 9 8 6 4
♡ 6
◊ 7
♣ Q J 10 6 5 3 2

South
♠ K 3
♡ Q J 10 8 3
◊ A J 8 3
♣ 8 4

If South fails to cash a high club before playing a third heart, West wins the third heart and plays a club, which dummy wins. Thereafter, declarer must guess how to exit safely from dummy. Declarer can exit dummy safely with a diamond. But if declarer attempts to exit dummy by playing the king and another club, West ruffs the king of clubs.

The dentist is upset again as we make Six Hearts, Doubled.

"How can you bid Four Spades with only a queen and a jack?" he yells at East. The dentist then challenges East to go out to the parking lot, where he can be taught a lesson on how to bid properly. East declines the dentist's challenge, but he quits the game. North and I also quit the game.

I make a mental note to never again play bridge with the dentist. Playing bridge is no fun at all when one of the players is belligerent.

Hand 59

THE COFFEE DRINKER

I've been drinking two cups of coffee a day, every day, since I was 18 years old. That amounts to 32,142 cups of coffee. In 1991, I began using an artificial sweetener in my coffee in lieu of sugar. I'll tell you about that later, dear reader.

Playing rubber bridge, partner and I bid to Four Hearts on the following auction:

The Bidding:

NORTH	EAST	SOUTH	WEST
—	—	2 ♣	Pass
2 ◊*	Pass	2 ♡	Pass
3 ♣**	Pass	3 ♡	Pass
4 ♡	Pass	Pass	Pass

*weak   **second negative

West leads the queen of diamonds:

North
♠ K J 10 8
♡ 10 6
◊ 6 5 4 2
♣ 7 6 5

South
♠ Q 9 2
♡ A K Q J 9 8
◊ A
♣ K 10 3

Four Hearts is an excellent contract. I have nine top tricks consisting of two spades, six hearts, and a diamond. I can lead a club to my ten and later a club to my king. This will enable me to win a tenth trick if the ace of clubs, or the queen jack of clubs, is at my right.

I can also make Four Hearts if my opponents win the ace of spades on the first or second round. Most likely, however, my opponents will duck the ace of spades twice. This will limit me to two spade tricks.

The challenge on this hand is to win a club trick when West holds the ace-queen or ace-jack of clubs. If I ruff three diamonds and then exit in spades, I can probably win a club trick no matter where the club honors are located.

I win the ace of diamonds, enter dummy with the ten of hearts and ruff a diamond. I continue with the ace and king of hearts, pitching a club from dummy. Both opponents follow to the second round of hearts. West shows void on the third heart, pitching a club.

I lead a spade to dummy's ten, which holds, and continue with another diamond ruff, East dropping the king and West the jack. I can't tell if the diamonds are divided four-four or five-three. But no matter how the diamonds divide, it's correct to ruff another diamond.

I continue with a spade to dummy's jack, which holds, and ruff another diamond with my last trump. Both opponents follow. With the diamonds breaking four-four, Four Hearts is cold.

I lead the queen of spades from hand to East's ace. If East plays a low club, I'll insert the ten. No matter who has the ace of clubs, I'll win a trick with the king.

East does his best by playing the jack of clubs which I cover with the king. West has nothing but clubs left. After winning the ace and queen of clubs, West leads the nine of clubs to my ten, so I make Four Hearts.

The complete hand:

North
♠ K J 10 8
♡ 10 6
♢ 6 5 4 2
♣ 7 6 5

West
♠ 6 5 4
♡ 5 2
♢ Q J 10 8
♣ A Q 9 8

East
♠ A 7 3
♡ 7 4 3
♢ K 9 7 3
♣ J 4 2

South
♠ Q 9 2
♡ A K Q J 9 8
♢ A
♣ K 10 3

Four Hearts also makes if the diamonds break five-three, provided West holds the ace of spades or East holds the ace of clubs.

In 1996, I became terribly ill. Symptoms of my ill health consisted of chronic fatigue, headaches, weight loss, low body temperature, lung infections, skin rashes, hemorrhaging inside my eyes, and episodes of blindness.

I was so fatigued that I spent 16 hours a day in bed. I lost 40 pounds. My body temperature was so low that I began wearing two sweaters in addition to an undershirt, shirt and jacket. And at least three days a week I went blind for an hour a day.

I went to numerous doctors. None helped. None of the doctors whom I saw had any training which would enable them to diagnose the cause of my poor health. None of the doctors I visited suspected that I had been poisoned.

Finally, after two years of ill health, a friend suggested that the cause of my ill health probably was the aspartame which was contained in the artificial sweetener I had been using.

I immediately stopped taking the artificial sweetener. I slowly regained my health. Even so, it was another two years before all of the symptoms of my ill health disappeared. Eventually, I fully regained my health, although I still have some vision problems.

If you have any doubts about the dangers of artificial sweeteners, dear reader, look up aspartame on the internet. You'll find numerous internet sites which will tell you:

1. ASPARTAME IS POISON.

2. ASPARTAME CAUSES CHRONIC FATIGUE.

3. ASPARTAME CAUSES BLINDNESS.

Hand 60

ANOTHER GAME BID AND MADE

Playing rubber bridge I find myself playing Four Spades on the following hand:

The Bidding:

NORTH	EAST	SOUTH	WEST
—	—	1 ♠	Pass
2 ♣	Pass	2 ♡	Pass
3 ♠	Pass	4 ♠	Pass
Pass	Pass		

North
♠ Q 5 4
♡ K Q
♢ K 9 3
♣ K 9 8 5 4

South
♠ K J 10 7 6
♡ A J 6 4
♢ 6 2
♣ A 7

West leads the queen of diamonds:

I let West win the queen and jack of diamonds and ruff the third diamond. I then lead the ten of spades from hand, which holds. How should I continue?

I have ten tricks consisting of four spades, four hearts, and two clubs. There should be no problem making Four Spades if the spades break three-two. The only thing I need worry about is a four-one spade split.

If I were to lead a spade to dummy's queen, then the opponent with four spades could duck the spade, win the next spade and play a diamond, forcing me to ruff, for down one. And if I were to win dummy's queen of spades and then play hearts, the opponent with four spades would make the nine of spades by ruffing a heart.

No, it's better to play another high spade from hand, saving the queen of spades in dummy. But first I must play two rounds of hearts. I cash dummy's king and queen of hearts and then lead a spade to my ten. If the spades break, I have ten tricks. Unfortunately, East shows void on the second spade.

West studies the ten of spades and considers his options. If West ducks the ten of spades, I will cash the king and ace of clubs and then play hearts from hand, making Four Spades. With dummy's queen of spades available for an overruff in hearts, West won't be able to set Four Spades if he ducks the second round of trumps.

West does his best by winning the ace of spades and leading a diamond, which I ruff in hand. West has two little trumps remaining, while I have a high trump in dummy and a high trump in hand. I lead the ace of hearts. If West follows or discards, I will pitch a club from dummy, then cash the king and ace of clubs and ruff my last heart with dummy's queen of spades.

West, however, ruffs the ace of hearts. No matter. I overruff with dummy's queen of spades, return to hand with the ace of clubs and play the king of spades, extracting West's last trump. The jack of hearts and dummy's king of clubs win the last two tricks, so I make Four Spades.

The complete hand:

North
♠ Q 5 4
♡ K Q
♢ K 9 3
♣ K 9 8 5 4

West
♠ A 9 8 2
♡ 7 3
♢ Q J 10 7
♣ J 6 3

East
♠ 3
♡ 10 9 8 5 2
♢ A 8 5 4
♣ Q 10 2

South
♠ K J 10 7 6
♡ A J 6 4
♢ 6 2
♣ A 7

    This line of play also succeeds if East holds four spades and East's distribution is 4-3-3-3, 4-3-4-2, or 4-4-3-2.

Hand 61

THE MOTHER

"Jim, it's pouring outside. Be sure and take an umbrella with you when you go out," says my mother.

"Mother," I respond, "I'm over fifty years old. Don't you think it's about time you cut the umbilical cord?"

"Never," she replies.

I follow my mother's advice and take an umbrella with me to the Cavendish West Club. Partner and I bid to Four Hearts on the following hand:

The Bidding:

NORTH	EAST	SOUTH	WEST
—	—	1 ♡	Pass
2 ♣	Pass	2 ♡	Pass
4 ♡	Pass	Pass	Pass

North
♠ 4 2
♡ 10 8 7
◊ A K 8
♣ K J 10 7 5

South
♠ A 5
♡ A Q J 9 3
◊ 7 6 5
♣ Q 9 8

West leads the Jack of Spades.

How should I play Four Hearts? The normal play is to win the ace of spades, enter dummy with the ace of diamonds and take the heart finesse.

If the heart finesse wins, I can pick up the hearts, force out the ace of clubs, pitch a diamond on the clubs, and make Four Hearts with an overtrick.

But if the heart finesse loses, my opponents will win the king of hearts, cash a spade, and lead a second diamond. Later, when I force out the ace of clubs, my opponents will win a diamond and I will be down one in Four Hearts.

The best play to make Four Hearts is to win the ace of spades and lead a low heart from hand, giving up on the heart finesse. With this line of play my opponents should be able to defeat Four Hearts only if the clubs divide four-one and they obtain a club ruff.

I lead a low heart from hand to dummy's seven, which wins. This is a better play than the ace and a heart, for a low heart will prevent me from losing control if the hearts divide four-one. I continue with a heart to my queen, which West wins. West leads a diamond, which I win with dummy's ace. I play the ace of hearts, extracting West's last trump, then force out the ace of clubs, so I make Four Hearts.

The complete hand:

North
♠ 4 2
♡ 10 8 7
♢ A K 8
♣ K J 10 7 5

West
♠ J 10 8 6
♡ K 5 2
♢ J 9 4
♣ A 6 2

East
♠ K Q 9 7 3
♡ 6 4
♢ Q 10 3 2
♣ 4 3

South
♠ A 5
♡ A Q J 9 3
♢ 7 6 5
♣ Q 9 8

After several hours of rubber bridge, I return to my condo. I have a telephone message from my mother telling me that my hair is too long and that I need a hair cut. If it's not one thing, it's a mother.